Praise for *The Writing on the Wall*

• "36 Best Indie Books Worth Discovering"
–*Kirkus Review 2023*

• "I thought this was incredibly interesting and
engaging. If you are a woman looking to be inspired
and want to break through your own glass ceiling,
this is the book for you." – *Nicole Pyles / Vine Voice*

• "While reading this well-written, engrossing, and
witty memoir, I often read bits of advice out loud to
my teenage daughter who enjoyed them as much as I
did. And honestly, if you can get a teenage girl to smile
you're knocking it out of the park. Very highly
recommended" – *Jamie Michele / Readers' Favorite*

• "It was an exciting, fast paced read – nearly
impossible to put down, and each time I did, I was
filled with excitement and anticipation for the next
moments I could steal time away from the demands of
life to pick it back up again!" – *Pam S., FL*

• "Marilyn's book does an excellent job of describing
how women are strong and complex when it comes to
decision making. Her memoir offers the world a real
perspective of women who challenged cultural norms
of her time and became successful even when facing
adversity." – *Lisa L., VA*

• "Candid, insightful page-turner." – *Janet L., NYC*

D0907622

THE WRITING ON THE WALL

by Marilyn Howard

ISBN 978-1-7333196-3-8
ISBN 978-1-7333196-2-1 (mobi edition)

Table of Contents

The Writing on the Wall

Chapter 1

The Beckoning Path

Movers are arriving tomorrow. There are still many crucial things to do. As I leave this seven-office suite in midtown Manhattan, I find some items are too large to bring. Tom Gong, my internet guru and tenant, will take the large copier and some furniture to his new location. I didn't realize back in 1994 that he would become the catalyst for a vision inspiring my later web business. An agreeable degree of excitement is in the air on this beautiful spring day.

I am accustomed to changes, but moves always evoke a lot of nostalgia. Physical items can be replaced—but not twenty years of memories. I will miss the friendly office companionship and laughter. We worked well as a team, and some fantastic talent walked through our doors. Now, significant contracts are ending, and new technology continues to change business in unanticipated ways. The time to heed warnings has come, so I'm taking the winnings and making changes. Not all dreams turn out as expected, but transformations always create new adventures.

I seemed born ready for adventure. A curiosity was ignited at birth, creating early memories, and as a youth, trails chosen at puzzling forks in the road gave the journey mysterious potential. Images stuck in my mind and created a yearning. I sought excitement and later plunged into the vast ocean of business—naively unaware of sharks and other ominous threats that lurked there. Nevertheless, I grew into a thriving entrepreneur and mother. I learned that being an entrepreneur can be a survive-or-die adventure. A game-changing storm can come up suddenly, or a fork in the road can lead to a dead end.

Perhaps it was in my genes or destiny to explore new paths and become a trailblazer. My grandfather was an entrepreneurial small businessman, and my father created patents owned by his employer. My generation certainly never expected innovation or running a business as the pathway for a woman.

"Doing it all" became the hope of women in the 1960s and 70s. Many women, including myself, were determined to reinvent themselves and restructure the opportunities offered to them by society. In many ways, they succeeded, but there continue to be unique issues for women in business. Their hurdles are very different than the experiences of their male counterparts. Mixing motherhood with a career or entrepreneurship requires a very reliable support system along with a good business plan, skill training, adequate start-up customers or investment capital, focus on priorities—and luck.

While growing up in the 1950s and 1960s is a different reality from today, women still face many of the same challenges. Fortunately, they have many more tools to work with and the experiences of earlier women entrepreneurs for guidance.

Determined that my destiny would not be the narrow path predicted for most girls of my time, I wanted to imbibe life in big gulps and longed for opportunities. Looking back over sixty years, my life tells the story of the women's movement and my entrepreneurial business is an example of a woman entering uncharted territory.

Without any women career mentors or business models, I stumbled and fell, but I got up again. My heartbeat became part of the movement that followed. We thought we could have it all, and I certainly broke the conventions.

After twenty-five years as an entrepreneur in business, I've learned that adapting to market and office changes with flexibility determines results. Men and women need the skill of reinventing with an upbeat attitude—both business and self. Interruptions in our plans wake us up to exciting new chapters.

The shifting life of an entrepreneur can be a wild ride. In the late 1980s, technology started to move at unprecedented rates. Even the giant Eastman Kodak never expected digital photography to take over so quickly. Today's entrepreneur is more alert to fluctuating markets. A small business has the advantage of adjusting swiftly, but only those entrepreneurs with enough flexibility to keep up with change stay in the winner's circle.

The stark truth about startups is that nobody knows clearly what they're doing. The ones who succeed learn quickly. Startups have to out-think and move faster than potential new competition—while keeping an eye on the horizon for new challenges. The goal is to keep moving forward in a winning direction through all the peaks and valleys. Play the game, and have fun.

Events converge, and influential people appear. Voices from the past speak their opinions. Sometimes simple sparks from a facial expression transfer an idea, create a magnetic attraction to a long-term relationship or empower personalities—igniting a sequence of events.

As the vision for my future appears and events move into place, important decisions become apparent. A street sign seems to point the way, or light beckons—showing the road to a life I seemed destined to live. The signs seemed "written on the wall," as in the famous Biblical phrase.

My self-aware mind appeared with incredibly early memories. Research done in the U.K. has affirmed that young infants can learn how to play with a toy without touching it, and half of those in the study remembered it four weeks later. It was concluded that even pre-verbal infants can encode, store and retain. What is generally thought of as "childhood amnesia" has remained a puzzle. The brain is rapidly changing during the early years, and there is plenty of room for memories. However, after age three and a half, a human's memory begins to forget. I remembered.

My early awareness ignited a curiosity about the soul and its interaction with the human body. I now know that deaf people have thoughts without language. Moreover, credible people have reported after-death and out-of-body experiences.

My childhood thoughts and the voices of my deceased grandparents are still vivid in my mind. Immediate family and friends played a foundational role in shaping growing questions and attitudes. Words and ideas reverberate for years.

At eighteen, a Fulbright Scholar from India, who had palm reading in his family for centuries, foretold a plot, which unwound over time. I tried to fight some predictions, knowing that no one can pick stocks or plan anything with absolute certainty.

However, events converged in an inescapable way, unexpectedly influencing significant decisions.

This book, like my life, is a hybrid of business and personal experiences. As I look back, my aspirations resulted from various intertwining components, but they began in memory with my grandparents' dreams and choices. Their tales of romance and intrigue were enchanting to my young ears.

At the stroke of midnight on New Year's Eve, as the century turned from 1899 to 1900, my grandparents married with the lights of press cameras flashing. At the age of twenty-two, Annie Waddilove married Will Witten, a handsome six-foot first-generation German man who was a year her junior and a sizeable contrast to her 5'2" height. The *Daily News* headlined it as the first wedding of the twentieth century with their picture and story on the first page.

Loving to dance and smitten by silent films, Annie dreamed of being in show business. Romance interfered with her ambitions for a movie career, so Annie translated those dreams into the dramatic timing of her wedding and having a show business family. Her five children, one of which was my mom, were raised to be theatrical stars with music and dance lessons, while she handmade all their artistically-designed costumes. She dreamed that her daughters would have a career and not marry young.

It was always fun exploring my grandparents' apartment years later. Their storage room was filled with tantalizing boxes of stage costumes. I tried them on and pranced about. Other rooms, furnished with intriguing turn-of-the-century furniture from a popular actress, had a romantic allure that fired up my imagination.

The family lived on the New Jersey shore, and life at the beach was fun for Anna, Edna, Bill, Margaret, and Len. Memories of their theatrical life and friends were part of many late dinner conversations.

In the 1920s, Edna, my mom, and her two sisters, Anna and Margaret, were all thin, pretty flappers and professional dancers. Some of their performances were in Vaudeville chorus groups— before the chorus line costumes came to be scandalously skimpy. Mom's older sister, Anna, had an enchanting voice and was her show partner in stage performances. They claimed some fame by performing several times in the legendary Palace Theater at Broadway and 47th in Manhattan—the most desired booking in the country. The Marx Brothers, Fanny Brice, and Ethel Waters were among its many stars. Margaret, the younger sister, was an incredible acrobat, and a dramatic photo of her in a backbreaking pose is a family treasure. Since show biz gigs were spotty, they all had "bread and butter" careers to supplement income. Margaret worked part-time as a beautician, while Edna and Anna were secretaries.

At eighteen, Mom met Ed Howard, my dad, an aspiring architect who also loved to dance. Edna and Ed became a team. The young generation loved the freedom felt on the dance floor. Jazz bands played at dance halls, while radio stations and phonograph records carried their tunes to listeners across the nation. The "Charleston," "Cake Walk," "Black Bottom," and "Peabody" were famous. In later years, Mom taught me the "Charleston," and Dad demonstrated the "Peabody."

Dad made a good living working in an architect's firm. He first purchased a motorcycle and then a Model T Ford. As a wild young buck who liked to take risks, he would stand on the handlebars of his motorcycle and ride it between streetcars. Somehow, he managed to entice Mom to fly with him in an early model, open cockpit double-wing airplane, where he stood up without any harness to take pictures. Knowing him as a very conservative man later in life, these daredevil acts seem entirely out of character. However, his driving often left us on the edge of the seat; it was a clue to the thrills of his perilous past life.

Since Grandma wanted all her daughters to have a career and not marry young, she convinced my mother to break off their relationship in her early twenties. Mom sadly followed her mother's wishes, but she would meet Ed again when destiny brought them together during the Great Depression.

Everyone rode the economic bubble until the devastating 1929 stock market crash. The nation's total wealth more than doubled between 1920 and 1929. After the Crash, however, Dad's few stocks went bust, and he was out of work. The future looked bleak.

No matter how hard one may work changes in the economy and world environments create an underlying uncertainty. Entrepreneurs are left to grapple with the consequences and decisions made by others. Stock market crashes, interest rates, regulation changes, wars, political elections, plus catastrophic disasters from storms, fires, and flooding, are just a few of the many events that have far-reaching effects.

Eight years after their break up, my mom and dad fatefully met at a funeral. They exchanged glances, and the romantic chemistry fired up again. Mom was

11

working as a secretary and dating a new man, but soon Ed and Edna became a team once again. She helped Dad get a job with her company, and the wedding followed. Dad worked his way into an unexpected career as a project engineer.

My parents felt lucky since one-quarter of all wage earners were out of work from the market crash and the Great Depression. In 1937, their first child, Ed Jr., was born, and they purchased a home in the outer New York City borough of Queens, where some farmland was being developed for housing. My father chose the first house built on a dirt road—at the top of a small hill. The road led to a stone-front two-story bungalow with a white picket fence. Finally, they had the home and family they had always wanted. A chicken coop was added to the garage. It opened into a wired yard area for the chickens to roam. Dad planted berry bushes and fruit trees. He had known poverty and never wanted to go hungry again.

In 1905, when Dad was only five, his father had died—leaving his mother, Mary, a first-generation immigrant wife, to struggle on her own to support a five-year-old child in Manhattan as a cook and housekeeper. Work was limited for a woman without much education, but she would have made a savvy businesswoman in a later generation. I have always admired strong women who can adapt to life's many challenges. That described both my grandmothers.

Dad remembered his mother as a bright woman who spoke several languages, including fluent German and some Yiddish. A shrewd negotiating "goy," she knew the shopkeepers in the downtown Jewish markets would consider it bad luck to turn away their first customer on Sundays. She arrived first, bargained in Yiddish, and got the best price. Mary clearly understood the importance of timing in a business deal.

Strong women don't allow others to limit their potential. They take challenges and turn them into opportunities. Traditionally, strong women supported their men—often holding the pieces together while the man got the glory of success. As the mother of his children, as his social secretary, cook, and advisor, many women kept their husband's life organized and his image intact. When left on her own to make her way in a harsh world, Mary had to bravely reinvent herself and not quit. Life was often a struggle—especially for women with children. Today, many powerhouse women come from humble backgrounds where they were born or flung by fate.

The early 1900s had no safety nets such as Social Security, unemployment insurance, or Medicaid. Their tenement on Third Avenue, where the 59th Street Bridge now stands, held memories of difficult times. Dad later told stories about a challenging life where he had to chip away the ice from the sink in the morning to get water. He shared another startling story of having his tonsils pulled out with pliers and no anesthetic.

Mary died of an unknown sickness in 1916, possibly at the beginning of the deadly flu epidemic of 1917. She was laid out on the couch in their apartment because funeral homes were too expensive. Dad was left to fend for himself on the streets of Manhattan at age sixteen, doing his best to avoid the local street gangs with their neighborhood rivalries. He had assorted small jobs—including lighting street lamps. Someone he had thought was a friend rented a room to him for a while but then stole his few possessions.

Stories of perseverance and resilience help us believe in ourselves. Remembering we all face difficult things allows us to be better employees, managers, spouses, parents, children, siblings, and human beings. Knowing that our family members triumphed over obstacles can give us the faith and hope that we will too.

Dad wisely chose survival over self-pity. Determined to pursue his dream of a family, he forged ahead with a career. While working during the day as an assistant in an architect's office, Dad went to night school at Cooper Union to study architecture. He also found time to enjoy himself at dance halls where he met my mother.

The intense building boom surrounding that original dirt road leading to my parent's new home was unimaginable. Lots were filled in, and the local golf course became St. John's University. The chickens in our backyard lasted until regulations changed. Suddenly, the backyard's fresh eggs and frequent chicken dinners stopped.

Mom was forty when I entered the world, six years after my brother.

Chapter 2

Awakening

A guiding light seemed to turn on at birth. It planted a determination in the soul of my being to retain images and related thoughts. Taking the responsibility seriously, I put them into a mental bank of snapshots. An active childhood filled the depository, keeping the resolve in practice.

My earliest memories imprinted as soon as I entered the world, with random, captured moments. Shadows loomed above my carriage, and people made sounds. Without words, I was very aware of their presence—although my sight was blurred. I chose that visual. Click. I just knew flashes were important to remember because I would forget as an adult.

Other visuals included being on a changing table, helplessly unable to control my body and thinking that being a tiny baby was a really boring part of life. Click. My brother laughed when the old-fashioned removable potty-seat on my high chair in the kitchen had to be changed. Click. Another time, he laughed outside the bathroom when I was being toilet trained. Why did he think it was so funny? I was just doing what it was time for my body to do. I also remember the neighbor's son, Loren, passing things to me through the slats of an old-fashioned wooden playpen. Then my first steps. Click. Click.

My very first memory is the most difficult to accept. I thought to myself, "The time is now," as I was being born. There was no feeling of pain, although I remember crying in the hospital room. I understood going forward had unknown risks, but wanted to go ahead. When I started nursing, there were two women present. They seemed amazed that I knew where to start. I wondered why the surprise for what seemed so normal.

A profound awareness of another dimension existed. Without having fear or being cognizant of death's whole meaning, I told myself not to be afraid of leaving this world again. I knew I had come from somewhere and would return.

Of course, I've wondered if all my early memories could be true, but I've concluded they were not my imagination. There are too many recollections from the first five years of my life with the recurring theme of telling myself to remember. Why did I want to remember? It seemed there should be a reason, but I wouldn't find an answer until much later in life.

Dancing lessons and performances helped keep memories vivid. Mom began my dancing classes very soon after reaching age three. The first tap dance lesson was in a small studio. We had to climb a couple of flights of stairs in an old building. The older students danced in the front room, while my class was in the back with kids a little older than myself. To be accepted, I successfully learned the time-step by imitating the teacher. In addition to tap dancing, there were soon lessons in acrobatics and ballet, plus I modeled whenever Mom could book a job. Within the year, I could also tap in toe shoes around my room as easily as walking. Sometimes, my mother and I stopped at the Woolworth's 5 & 10 cent store lunch counter for a BLT sandwich on the way to a lesson, which was a special treat.

Recitals and performances were immense fun. Applying a little make-up or having my hair curled with a curling iron in a dressing room before performances were always thrilling. The dressing room contained a long mirror with chairs in front, where the parents fussed with their child's preparations. At a memorable Boy Scout's Father and Son Luncheon, our class did a tap and "wiggle" dance routine in red hula skirts, which was totally acceptable in this male-dominated world. I'm sure there were pedophiles then, probably more than today. Another time we performed a tap dance in bunny costumes.

Although I never learned why, I saw Mom cry in a dance class dressing room after a dispute with my teacher. It seemed to be a turning point. When kindergarten started, Mom sadly said, "I wanted to keep up the family tradition, but I don't have the energy needed to continue dance lessons." She was in her mid-forties with two children. Disappointed, I accepted her decision and looked forward to kindergarten.

All the lessons stopped, but my love of dance remained. Music and dancing would continually bring relaxation and smiles, even when times were rough.

On the first day of kindergarten, many kids were crying as their mothers left them alone for the first time. Accustomed to being on my own and giving recitals before large rooms of people, I adapted quickly to the classroom and pitched in, telling the other children not to worry as their mothers would be back later. The adults thought it was quite cute.

We lived with the threat of war. The Cold War with Russia could cause a nuclear bomb attack. Air raid sirens would go off. Even when hiding under a desk for an air raid test or putting on a "dog-tag" so we could be found after the strike, we viewed our early school experiences as predictable and secure. All cooperated as if it was a game, where those hiding under our desks would be the winners.

Chauvinism and inequalities were the accepted customs in the 1950s. Gender-based attitudes, actions, and abuses persisted, with only one role for women informing TV programs, policy decisions, and social customs. During WWII, many women joined the workforce to support the military. However, in the 1950s, they were urged to return to their roles as wives and mothers. Expectations of rigid stereotypical sex roles were supported on popular TV shows like "Ozzie and Harriet," "Father Knows Best," and "I Love Lucy."

If born a man, I might have become an engineer or computer programmer, but that was not an acceptable pursuit for a girl. While my brother was encouraged, I could just watch what were considered to be men's skills. Prince Charming supposedly would take care of all those tasks as well as pay the bills. As it turned out in later years, my husband would leave all repairs to me or the hired help. I was also told, "A girl's driving will only be in case of an emergency. It will be your husband's decision when and where you can drive later." Mostly because of my gender, Dad never let me drive a family car except to get a license.

18

Technology must have been in my genes. In later years, I would be very early among my peers to use technology and even did some computer programming. If only I had invested in those stocks! A stockbroker discouraged buying several of my suggestions, such as Apple, which became winners. I owned the first personal cell phone among contemporaries, and not investing in it was my mistake.

"Look but don't touch" was the policy for a woman in a man's world. Dad's fascinating basement workshop was filled with woodworking tools, electronics and his collection of amateur ham radios. I liked to watch him work there and on our old 1939 Buick—kept in the driveway as a second car well into the fifties. Driving this outmoded, dark-green car with straw seats down the street attracted neighborhood boys, who would try to jump and stand on the running board for a ride.

I craved challenging activities, but found the elementary school curriculum boring after learning to read. Videos and computers didn't exist. Interesting projects were rare. In the fifth and sixth grades, I read the class reading assignments from our textbook and completed the chapter questions within the first few weeks. Instead of getting something new, I was excused from future class assignments and participation. Boredom in my youth drove me to want a different life. A lack of enjoyable stimulation leads to a craving for relief.

Even girls' sports were boring. The skills encouraged in girls downplayed their abilities. Games were modified to keep girls from getting too aggressive. They were only allowed three basketball dribbles before passing it to another player. Most of the competition and action were eliminated. Cooperation was taught, but valuable competitive skills were lost. Fortunately, I had many years of street games with boys.

The friendly neighborhood boys were a good balance for the world's chauvinism and my brother, who teased me unmercifully. Cross-training for motherhood and a man's business role started early. Learning about "fight to win" was early resilience training needed later in business.

Half of the week, I was a tomboy who played war games, handball and stickball. I also loved climbing through backyard fantasy jungles exploring with the local boys. An old fortified refrigerator box served as a group fort through snowstorms and rain. Each day, we enacted whatever scenes filled our imaginations. I was undaunted by the constant scraped knees and scratches. I discovered boys could be gross, and I was sometimes squeamish when it came to bugs or blood, but the excitement and competition kept me coming back. The adventures were exhilarating.

On other days I joined the girls for the more ladylike roles of playing dolls, hopscotch and jump-rope. Adventures seemed much more enticing than homemaking. Both worlds were full of fantasies that could be enjoyable, but my allowed future of homemaker grew boring after a few days. I wondered, "Could I find a life that wouldn't limit a woman's role?

I didn't know then, but a double life playing or operating in two environments prepares for many useful business skills. Current corporations sometimes provide cross-training for positions, and small businesses need people cross-trained to fill in when others are absent.

"First, you have to learn the rules of the game, and then you have to play better than anyone else." Albert Einstein.

Running a business is often correlated to playing sports, with good reason. Players learn the rules, hit hard and go for all the bases. Competition is encouraged. Our game of streetball was played with baseball rules—but utilized tennis or rubber balls to prevent breaking windows. Girls were welcome if capable of hitting the ball and getting to first base.

In the days before video games, good weather found everyone outdoors, only returning home for meals. Other entertainment included bike riding, roller skating, handball in the park, and whatever else triggered our energies. In the winter, snow brought kids from neighboring blocks for sledding on our big hill. At least, it was the highest in the area. The hill appeared very flat from an adult's perspective years later. The size of a hurdle depends upon attitude.

A neighborhood mother invited anyone interested in congregating to play the card game of Canasta in her backyard on summer evenings. Assorted card games plus board games like "Monopoly" filled our open hours. To fill time alone, I would play "Solitaire."

Until I was seven, my brother often provoked profuse tears. My tears would frequently produce Mom's warning, "Laugh, and the world laughs with you. Cry and you cry alone." I got tougher by deciding not to be a "cry-baby" anymore and holding the tears inside. A mental note of age seven as the decision time was captured for the memory bank.

Obviously enjoying power and control, my brother continued to hurt my feelings, physically poke or trip me, and orders me around. Why did he want to control me? With time, I stayed fixed to my preferred thoughts and resisted. In later years, I would meet other controlling men.

My mother said, "Your brother is just a normal, active boy and will outgrow it." Although an unequal match, as long as I didn't get physically hurt, my parents believed that we should solve our own disputes—a major mistake. Tact and self-control is a necessity for business as well as life. He never learned when his opinions weren't wanted. Sensitivity training was needed.

A few years ago, when a therapist friend asked about my early memories of men, I vaguely recalled my father in the background—while my brother was a frequent tormenter. She commented that this first lesson in self-absorbed men played a part in accepting insensitive behavior later in life.

A trip to the beach almost had a disastrous ending. Jones Beach had a wide expanse of sand with giant waves. A colossal ocean breaker came crashing down, sweeping me off my feet and dragging me out to sea. I was sure I was drowning. As the bubbles floated up, my early memories of another dimension were a comfort. I wondered why I was being taken so young. Suddenly, my father's strong hand grabbed me, and I was pulled to safety. Swimming lessons soon followed.

At age eleven, events converged to form my mission statement in life. Older parents, an aunt's early death and my grandmother's depression came together to make me think about life-altering events, the shortness of a lifespan, and the ravages of old age. It reinforced a resolve to cram as much into my good years as was possible and led to planning how I would achieve my goals.

As a young child, I enjoyed hearing my mother laugh and reminisce about her earlier years with her older sister and Vaudeville partner, my Aunt Anna. Anna's life had taken an unexpected turn. She had dreams of stardom but fell in love and planned to get married around the time of Mom's engagement. She was converting to Catholicism to marry a Roman Catholic man, but tragically, Anna's fiancé died from a slow, creeping mustard gas poisoning contracted in WWI. After his death, she didn't think she could ever love again, so she married the church, becoming Sister Mary Honora.

Game-changing events seem to come into life, whether ready or not to receive them. The stark contrast between the colorful world of song and dance and the restricted world of the convent created questions in my mind about powerful life changes. Instead of the music and dance she loved, her assignment was to be an x-ray technician in a hospital. The sight of blood was distasteful, but she dutifully did the job for many years.

When I was nine, the first signs of cancer appeared on my mother's younger sister. Aunt Margaret's hands developed an undiagnosed rash, triggered by the harsh chemicals used without wearing rubber gloves as a beautician. Diagnosed later as skin cancer, it had already spread to her breast. After Margaret's death, her three-year-old daughter, Ginny, was left in Mom's care. I missed my aunt, but loved having a new toddler in the house. I was her big sister for a year and motherhood seemed more appealing. Then Ginny's father remarried and Ginny left as quickly as she had come. I sadly saw her only occasionally after that, until we were much older.

Grandma's pain and depression over Margaret's death were incomprehensible. She wanted to die before anything terrible happened to her other offspring. A complete reversal of the dynamic woman I had known happened at only age seventy-three. How could I avoid depression happening to me? I had loved Grandma's energy and fascinating stories about show business. Her depression reinforced a desire to live life to its fullest and avoid despair.

The remedy for grandma was thought to be warm weather and a move to Miami, Florida, where her son Bill had a pleasant small guesthouse in the backyard of his home. The change didn't revive her spirit. Margaret was gone; all her memorabilia, her home of many years and her other family members were left up north. These connections and memories were her deeply personal ties to life.

The new Danish Modern style of furniture was fashionable but uninteresting to me. Much to my chagrin, the beautiful old furnishings collected from an actress around the turn of the century were chopped up for firewood. I hoped grandma didn't know it was happening. The elegant old sideboard and china cabinet were considered worthless, but I knew that it was a mistake. I would not let that happen to my parent's bedroom set, which I fondly cherished. Events often teach lessons about what we don't want to happen in our lives.

Depression seemed such a waste. I wanted the woman who had enthusiastically applauded at my dance recitals to still be there for me. Her body didn't die until age 80. Grandpa died of a quick heart attack while out on his daily health walk a few years later.

The quick way, with a positive attitude, was definitely preferable.

At age eleven, the numerous card and board games that I played with the neighborhood kids generated thoughts about the game of life. Trying to get around the board or win a card game converged with thoughts about our life journey. What would be the best way to avoid remorse in old age? In life and games, a lot depends upon the role of the dice and the cards that are dealt. I knew my choices would be limited. "Play the cards the best way possible" became my mission statement.

In subsequent years, the phrase provided decision-making strength. There is sometimes no easy answer. Amid numerous challenges, lawsuits and family fluctuations, that statement was a steadying thought. A mistake in business can cost a lot of money, and steady nerves are needed.

Chapter 3

Growing Pains

Preteen and teen years are a time of dreams, imagination, new opportunities, and questions. As I danced around my room on Saturday mornings listening to Dick Clark's top 100 songs on the radio, I imagined a life of adventures beyond dull suburbia. I didn't want a boring adult life, and I certainly didn't get one. It was a dream without specific goals. There was no way to visualize the amazing adventures to come.

"Of course I remember you." It was forty years later when I reached out to my best friend from childhood. Activities separate relationships, and then the years pass too quickly. We shared many happy memories of childhood and our love of art. Occasional visits to my friend Joyce's summer home in the Catskill Mountains were idyllic times of youth, absorbing and enjoying nature. We would wander in the woods, smelling the fresh air and picking the blueberries that her mother would serve with sour cream for a snack or in blueberry pancakes for breakfast the next day. Wildflowers were identified and saved. Wild salamander babies were picked up by their tails and put into shoeboxes with traces of natural dirt and leaves, so we could study their habits. It was fascinating to see a resourceful salamander's ability to regenerate a limb, tail or eye from an injury.

Our love of art later evolved into career skills for both of us. French class calendars and historical shadow box displays were our specialties. Display figures were made with pipe cleaners wrapped in sticky paper maché made from flour, water and paper towel strips, then painted flesh tones. Her mother had worked in textiles and provided scraps of attractive fabric that she had around the house for their costumes. They were charming displays that everyone admired and were fun to make.

We were classmates, after-school playmates and regular study buddies. Joyce had one of the top IQs in my class and would helpfully work through my questions or explore finding answers. I admired her ability and willingness, even though she said it was a good way for her to review for exams. Our middle school Special Progress class stayed together for two years with a curriculum covering the 7th, 8th, and 9th grades. It was a huge, much-needed change from grade school. Those years were critical for developing good work habits. It made me feel empowered and became my stimulus for wanting a college education. Women were treated as equals, a stark contrast to the chauvinism encountered elsewhere. I assumed the high school would be similar to that class.

My parents' attitude was bewildering. They said an advanced class would probably be difficult, so I shouldn't accept. I had to argue my point, and they reluctantly conceded. Their thinking was largely colored by the fact that girls shouldn't outshine boys, and it would make me older than most of the boys in my grade. Mom cautioned, "There will be fewer men available if you aim too high."

Becoming a woman didn't sound like it would be much fun. Instead of praise, I often received cautions that meant "don't try to beat men in a man's world." My parents thought the NY State Regent's tests must have been much easier than when my brother took them, since I received better scores. Even when he confirmed they were the same questions, the message was clear: I shouldn't outshine him. Mom also warned, "Men's egos are very important to their manhood, so should be respected." That was okay with me, but I wanted my ego respected as well.

The qualities encouraged in young girls then and now can unintentionally make women downplay their own worth. It can be a struggle to find a personal professional voice, to rise above social expectations and the fear of failure.

I wanted to escape being trapped in the women's role that sometimes encircled me. I didn't want the same life that had created depression in some of the women in my family.

As I became more independent, Mom became depressed because she felt her role as a mother was almost over. First, it was Grandma, and now her. I wondered how I could stop this terrible downhill spiral. With encouragement, Mom found outside activities and became happy to be needed again. I definitely didn't want to feel useless after my children were grown, so I would try to find a life that always offered new vistas and learning experiences.

Mid-summers could be very quiet, as most kids went to summer camp or away with family. I was often bored and relentlessly begged my father to take us on a vacation. He began taking us on driving trips during his two-weeks off each summer. It was a start, but I was anxious to explore more of what was out there.

To spend time away during the hot summer, I volunteered as a free babysitter and dishwasher for my aunt and uncle, who had two active sons, ages two and four. They traveled to state parks in a small sixteen-foot travel trailer for most of the summer. We parked next to the tents and other small trailers. After chores, there were hours of fun by the lake and in the recreation hall with other teenagers. Then, in a flash, the fleeting flirtations of summer were over.

The reality of limitations and making money grew. Prince Charming was supposed to take care of my family bills, but could I be sure? Would he make enough money to support the style of living that I craved? Trying to be responsible with money came early.

People who tell you money isn't important are often those who have given up on making it or those who have someone else as their support. While putting money ahead of relationships and ruthlessly stepping on others to get it is cruel, unethical and damaging, the necessity to pay for the basic costs of living is real.

Babysitting employment started at age eleven and filled most of my weekends for several years. The financial independence was exhilarating. I enjoyed the freedom that came with making money and chose to purchase most of my own clothes because I had different tastes from my mother. Of course, we had to agree on major purchases like a new coat, and they covered any school expenses.

"You can't keep your money under a mattress. Inflation will come and steal it," warned Dad when I complained my childhood savings wouldn't buy much. He added, "Savings have to get interest from a bank."

I later learned that inflation happens because the government prints and borrows more money than it has. Without inflation, they would be limited by what the public allowed in taxes. While there are benefits to the government controlling interest fluctuations, inflation can have harmful effects by creating imaginary increases in demand, distorting business behaviors. The dotcom era's historic, speculative internet bubble, fueled by relatively low interest rates and available capital, would later affect my business aspirations.

At fourteen, I wanted a better paying job, but local stores had enough candidates from the regular workforce and didn't need to hire minors like myself. Minors under sixteen needed special working papers with restrictions set by the state to prevent child labor abuse. I applied for an after-school job at Woolworth's in the downtown Manhattan financial district at a friend's suggestion. They were recommended as willing to accept government papers that specified only part-time work and job would not interfere with school. I looked around at all the tall buildings in Manhattan and wondered, "Is it possible for me to find a well-paying job in New York City's center of business, someday?"

It was a long subway ride to work in Manhattan, and the trip was a revelation. Every car had at least one well-dressed, dirty old businessman who tried to rub against me. At first, I thought it was an accident, but then I realized what was happening. I did my best to avoid the situation, looking for women to stand next to, or putting objects in between the man and myself, and when all else failed, just ignoring it. I was too shy to make a scene, which is what they wanted. A one-way commute required a twenty-minute bus ride—followed by at least forty-five minutes of standing on a subway car. Sometimes it also included train transfers—depending on the time of day. It was tedious, but my only answer to making the minimum wage.

Money is a powerful motivator. It buys financial independence and brings a focus to priorities. The business person has to identify and focus on the money-makers of the company. In my business, there always seemed to be a top ten.

As a young teen, my focus and first necessary big purchase was the new invention of contact lenses. Vainly, I had walked around half-blind for years, only wearing eyeglasses to see the blackboard or read. I couldn't see facial expressions or read signs and was lucky I didn't get hit by a car. With my vision at 20/600, everything was a blur. A close buddy had to tell me what was happening. Glasses felt like a death sentence and only worn in class. I worried it would make me unattractive. Adding to the problem, I continually read books in poor light. I read about contacts in a magazine, and my money was saved for the purchase.

I was excited to be the first among my contemporaries to get hard lenses; soft lenses were not invented yet. From then on, the world opened up, and the lenses would only be out of my eyes when sleeping. While not seeing was an isolating experience, seeing clearly created acrophobia. Steep drops were terrifying.

Gradually, I became accustomed to a newly visible world. As I embarked on the rock and roll era of my teenage years, many colorful adventures followed. Elvis Presley's first single, "Heartbreak Hotel," was released in January 1956, and it was the number-one hit as I began high school that September.

Chapter 4

Coming of Age in the Late 1950s

Chauvinism grew into social divides. Clicks formed, and limitations developed. It was cool to be like everyone else. That hasn't changed much, although fashions today pretend to be an expression of independence. While I was not the first teenager to find fault with high school and want to get on with life, I felt that way.

Women were definitely not mentored for a management career at Jamaica High. They were submerged in the masses and expected to survive. I had looked forward to high school, but I found it a graduation factory. There were over 1200 students in my senior class. They put me into classes with no connections to my good friend Joyce or other earlier classmates, resulting in lost enthusiasm for school.

All students could choose from three high school curriculums: college-bound academics, secretarial skills, or the trades. Mom encouraged the secretarial diploma, which would work well with raising a family. I chose the academic course of study for potential college-bound students.

Aspiring to attend college, I followed my mission statement and worked hard to receive high grades, but the excitement and confidence were gone. I was uncomfortable in front of large groups of people and hated giving graded oral reports. My hands shook and my voice quivered. My sentences formed best without distractions. Sensitivity to everything going on in the room disrupted my focus, leading to nervousness. I was in good company, but I didn't know it then. Warren Buffet, Thomas Jefferson, Abraham Lincoln, George Seinfeld, and Frederic Chopin struggled with performance anxiety and stage fright. It is one of the most common phobias.

Public speaking is an important skill to develop. Later in life, I declined many public speaking opportunities because of my insecurities in front of groups. My school was sink or swim, and the large classes could be overwhelming. A smaller, more nurturing class structure or a girl's school might have made a big difference.

Schools put a lot of emphasis on college entrance, but soft skills are needed for success in business and life. Entrepreneurs often see the grand vision, but slip and fall over the small stuff along the way. Also known as "transferable skills," many soft skills work everywhere. They include communications, emotional intelligence, teamwork, flexibility and time management. By the end of high school, students should be enabled with the necessary self-confidence to navigate their environment, work well with others, and achieve their dreams through a career or further education. Practical math like budgeting, hazards of creating debt and job searching skills are also essential to managing life.

In life and business, you're trying to develop a presence to connect with and inspire others. You want to build trust and credibility, plus be clear and energetic. You want your seat at the table to count. This type of presence does not come from perfect gestures and report content. The ability that propels careers and builds followers comes from the inside out. In the end, much of the presenter's style has to be individual. However, self-confidence needs to be encouraged with positive reinforcement, not graded. Emotions can be regulated with logic and practice. Experience will triumph over fear.

Self-esteem fuels personal development, good work habits, determination and eventual success. However, insecurities, abuse and neglect will become troublesome baggage. Bad habits begin early. Encouragement, mentors and family support prepare the adult personality for life's later challenges. We constantly reinvent and adapt in a search for the right mix of skills to thrive.

Teaching methods and curriculum in the 1950s were without attractive visual aids. Moreover, papers had to be manually typed, with copies made by placing carbon paper between the bond papers on the typewriter. Erasing a typo required manually erasing under the carbon copies. There was no cut and paste, so editing was laborious. It was easy for students to quickly get discouraged.

As in my younger years, I walked between two worlds. In high school the division was between religious affiliations rather than gender. All my classes, each comprised of about thirty pupils, were organized by merit and mainly high-achieving Jewish students. Otherwise, diversity was a natural part of life, and I didn't encounter any prejudice among students. The high school was about a third black from South Jamaica. Most Catholics attended private religious schools. I was a member of the only Protestant church within miles, and white Protestants were the minority for my first twelve grades. I never knew otherwise until I went to college.

Both my Jewish and Protestant friends had separate parties and interests. I enjoyed attending both and understood the boundaries. Jewish boys weren't allowed to ask me out, and if you intended to marry a Catholic, you would have to convert. I was supposed to date and marry a Protestant. While I was never aware of any discrimination, no one I knew ever tested the limitations. Dating was expected and accepted to be within racial and religious borders.

My questioning mind asked, "Why?" to many circumstances. Mom usually responded with timeless wise quotes to answer problems, but I wanted actual demonstrations or justifications based on real-life experiences.

Although Mom's sayings were simplistic, they stuck in my mind—often guiding my actions. In later years, I would find them on my lips for a fast answer.

When I complained, she said, "It's never so bad it couldn't be worse."

When my brother and I fought, she advised, "Two wrongs don't make a right."

When I was frustrated looking for a job, she urged, "If at first you don't succeed, try, try again."

When I wanted an exciting life, "God helps those who help themselves."

When I contemplated life, "There will always be people better off and worse off in life, so learn to be happy with whom you are."

When I was upset, "Laugh, and the world laughs with you. Cry and you will cry alone."

When I thought about whom I might marry, "When you make your bed, you lay in it."

There were many more. One that I still question is "Everything happens for a reason."

What were the reasons? Why do bad things happen? Organized religions had different answers. The answer from my early memories was that we are just passing through, but I wanted a more detailed explanation. A higher power seemed obvious.

My questions about scripture prophecy and self-determination produced a circular and seemingly inadequate answer from my minister. If prophets could forecast the future, do we really have a choice?

Youth wants action, solutions and purpose. No one seemed to have clear answers, but I expected future events would provide a better explanation. I thought, "Someday, I'll figure it out and maybe write my own book on life and love."

I wanted adventures and wondered, "How could they be achieved?" A woman's fun, prime years before marriage seemed a short span, so needed to be maximized. Was my only hope finding a Prince Charming who would rescue me? Mom had accepted her fate as a normal life for a woman, but I wanted more than socializing with relatives and having coffee and cake with neighbors. It would have to be a different prince who could make me live happily ever after.

Of course, Dad got out of the house by going to work all week, but Mom didn't. Mom's rationale would be, "A woman's support role as a wife at home is very important." She was right for some women, but the pattern didn't transpire for everyone.

Many years later, a man told me, "Men need just one trusted woman, but women have a larger need for socialization beyond the man." He added that men generally only confide in that one woman, mostly talking sports, business and jokes to other men.

My main fun memory of Dad was his ability to dance. He brought my brother and me to his yearly business dinner dance for several years. I couldn't understand why my "fun Dad" only appeared about once a year. The responsibilities of marriage had changed him, and it seemed to be related to saving money for our education, any potential emergencies and his retirement. He felt the role of a good father was being a stable provider—something he never had as a child. His childhood had left deep scars. I admired him for surviving difficult times but wanted his touch. With adolescence came the yearning for an affectionate companion.

As I sat on the couch next to Dad watching "Father Knows Best" or "Ozzie and Harriet" portray the perfect families on TV, I curled up next to him, wanting his arm put around me. He never would, even when I asked. I would lift his arm up and drag it around me, and he would still pull away. I couldn't understand what held him back. My mother said it was because he never had affection as a child. That reason didn't stop me from feeling a sense of rejection. It just wasn't his style. He showed love in his own way and would thoughtfully buy heart-shaped boxes of chocolates on Valentine's Day for my mother and me, and he never forgot birthdays.

His inability to show physical affection probably hindered my mother's sex life. Occasional overheard comments made me think she considered sex mostly an unpleasant marital duty. Mom would take a deep breath and say to him tensely and without enthusiasm, "Okay, Tuesday is the night." Watching TV was the only thing they did on most weeknights, and I knew they weren't talking about TV. On another occasion, when I mentioned that I thought sex was supposed to be enjoyable, she said, "Sometimes. You'll find out."

I wondered, "What becomes of falling in love and romance?"

While at my aunt and uncle's house, I realized what was wrong. Their dog was hugging a toy on the floor in the middle of the living room. Somebody commented that the dog thought the toy was his girlfriend. My father's response was, "If it was his girlfriend, he wouldn't hug it so long." We all looked at him in silence, but he didn't get it. I realized that I wasn't the only one not getting enough hugs, and thought it was probably the reason for Mom's lukewarm attitude toward sex.

Affection matters. Men may think it is their role to be macho and tough, but women I've known want displays of affection. Most men are capable, but their needs can be different. They may require coaching to get your warmth. Otherwise, women often aren't satisfied.

My brother was beyond cold. We never communicated as friends during our childhood, and I can't think of anything we ever had in common other than family. During my teenage years, he could no longer hold me by the feet upside down until I screamed for mercy. Although just an annoyance to me, he grew into a six-foot, attractive-looking guy with dark brown hair and a good physique from bodybuilding and gymnastics. Our old-style party line was a conference call between all devices without being invited. Girls would call; they became my chance to get even. I would retaliate by sneaking on the extension phone, to interrupt or tease about the conversation later.

Dad cautioned, "Think for yourself. Don't just conform." He warned, "Cigarettes teach conformity and are bad for your health." Dad was a non-smoker. Cigarettes were advertised as glamorous, so most teens fell into line by smoking at parties and elsewhere. Dad tested my character by inviting me to smoke in front of him. If I was weak enough to smoke and not have self-control, it would form his opinion for other situations. Thankfully, the method worked, and he convinced me never to start the addictive dependency. Occasionally, I avoided a scene by following Dad's wise suggestion to just take the cigarette to the lips and not inhale. Groupthink was not something to be admired, but occasional faking seemed a harmless compromise.

Chapter 5

Launch into Adulthood

My high school years during the late 50s were accurately depicted by the musical comedy *Grease*. Boys wore leather jackets, and Elvis Presley's hairstyles were pasted with grease products. The popular "ski jump" hairstyle had a high puff of hair slicked into place at the front of a boy's head. When the fad started, sideburns were considered rebellious. Tight skirts for girls replaced early 50s hoop skirts. The Rock & Roll era had begun, dramatically changing the future of popular music.

The cool group drove around in colorful convertibles asking girls if they wanted a ride. Hanging out on street corners and going for car rides with unknown local guys may seem dangerous, but the neighborhood scene attracted only local teenagers and was not infiltrated by pushers. Beer was the only liquor available, and I hated the taste. Some guys occasionally had a few too many or pushed limits. However, problematic situations were generally

41

obvious to detect, so danger could be avoided, plus I always traveled with a friend.

A casual hangout was a pizza parlor where teens played the jukebox. At other times, we would chat at the corner store lunch counter—drinking chocolate egg cream sodas, which contained neither eggs nor cream.

Parties and social life were an escape from boring class work. Only a few more years and we would be old enough to marry, get a job or go to college. My party girlfriend, Jeanie, was a fun and attractive, sometimes coquettish, sometimes comical companion. Her entertaining antics and sex appeal often made her the center of attention for the boys. Her slapstick at parties included spilling drinks and bumping into people. We often organized small parties and taught the boys how to dance the "Swing" or "Stroll." As a pretty blond with a sense of humor and no shyness, she was fun to hang around with, and we frequently double-dated. While not possessing her classic model face, I had grown to a 5' 7" teenager with a slender frame and ash-blond hair.

I was her "straight man." To make my calm demeanor more exciting, Jeanie nicknamed me "Stormy." While it was sometimes hip to be raucous and colorful in high school, having the composure to weather storms served me well in life and was needed for running a business.

In the 1950s, the average age of first marriage was 20 years for women and 23 years for men. I knew many girls who got married soon after high school. My family had a long history of marrying late, so there was no family pressure to marry early, but marriage was expected as the natural course of life.

On Senior Prom night, girls dressed in their prettiest party dresses, while the boys rented tuxedos and presented wrist corsages to their dates. Wide, fluffy skirts were still in vogue, but I chose a classic cocktail dress with spaghetti straps and subtle lilac print, which would still be wearable today. A rented stretch limousine transported us to the prom at a Manhattan hotel. After the official prom with dinner and dancing, we dropped in on all the famous nightclubs, leaving the limo waiting outside. When the clubs closed, we rode the Staten Island Ferry until dawn. The goal was to stay up all night without sleep.

With everyone dressed for a senior prom, it was obvious that many of us were under the official drinking age of 18. Fake ID was never questioned. When I was in my twenties, I was asked more for proof and was still carded until age twenty-eight. The chauffeur prevented drunk driving.

Dick, my boyfriend for a couple of years and my Senior Prom date, was handsome and fun, but we knew separate lives would follow graduation. At the end of senior year, I began dating Van, a star in our high school musical, who was a grade behind. Dating Van continued during my visits home from college, and we attended his prom the following year.

Both were fun guys who provided lots of hugs, but I wasn't in love. The morals of the times were "nice girls" didn't have sex 'til marriage, and I wanted my future soul mate to respect me. The dating rules were clear. The boy's role was to be aggressive, and the girl's job was to say "No." The fairy tale ending was ever-present. I would marry a considerate, admirable man, and we would live a wonderful life, where all expenses would be his. My family expected me to pay my own way until marriage, but then, unquestionably, finances would be taken care of by my husband-to-be.

It's been said that the biggest danger is not that our hopes are too high; it is that they are too low. Although I was told there was the risk of becoming an "old maid," my dream was undeniable. I had forged ahead with hope for some form of higher education but didn't know if my family would let me go away to a university.

The generally-acceptable careers for a woman were home economics, nursing, music, art, or teaching. My favorite pastime of art was chosen for study. I planned to become a fashion illustrator. Art was not a financially-stable career goal for a man, but okay for me. I considered several NYC art schools and the Syracuse University Graphic Arts program.

Upon hearing that I was accepted by Syracuse, my art teacher, Naomi Miller, told me not to think twice. "If your father allows it, take the university education." She had a twinkle in her eye that made it indisputable.

Fortunately, Dad believed strongly in educational opportunities and had sacrificed to save for them. He agreed that good grades deserved a university. Not having degrees had closed doors for him, and Dad wanted to give us every chance possible within his reach. While it was considered a must for men and an option for women, he wouldn't deny me a university education. The awkward years were over, the work paid off, and my hope was realized. I was thrilled with the launch path to my adult life.

High school graduation in 1960 was at age 16, shortly before my 17th birthday. I had entertained myself during high school but was very ready to leave suburbia and move on to the pending new adventure of

Syracuse University. Getting a "MRS" degree may have been the ultimate goal for my family, but not me. I dreamed of seeing and doing everything possible, then of pursuing a career in Manhattan.

Chapter 6

University Insights

The 1960s were years when many Americans believed they were standing at the dawn of a golden age. During my time at Syracuse, the handsome and charismatic John F. Kennedy became president of the United States. A year later, I waited tensely with my friends while he had to face down a close atomic bomb attack in the Cuban Missile Crisis. The next year, when he was assassinated, we were all overcome with sadness and disbelief. Kennedy's confidence that government could possess the big answers to big problems lived on and seemed to set the tone for the rest of the decade. However, that golden age never materialized. On the contrary, by the end of the 1960s, it seemed that the nation was falling apart with civil rights conflicts, war protests, feminists burning their bras, and government crises. It started out with high hopes but ended with the 1969 Woodstock music festival calling for harmony and peace.

Arriving at the University, I was immediately amazed and excited when finding a new world of contemporaries from all over the country. The incoming freshmen were greeted for orientation week by the Goon Squad—sophomore students in orange caps and shirts who helped us unpack and would answer questions. Their job throughout the year was to spread school spirit around the campus, a tradition since 1944. The activities included leading football game cheers and putting on an annual Goon Show.

Music and excitement filled the halls as we emptied our suitcases. My assigned art and music women's dormitory was Hayden Hall, a funky four-story building with no elevators, student artwork on the walls and pianos in many of the rooms. The top, fourth floor, was the least desirable because of the flights of stairs necessary to reach it, so it was reserved for freshmen. Telephones were only in the main lobby, necessitating constant running up and down the stairs.

One of the black girls on our floor was dating the famous football legend, Ernie Davis. Next to my room was an aspiring Broadway theater musician who entertained with show tunes and her own compositions. Listening to the talented student musicians was a delight. In 1971, our landmark dorm was demolished and replaced by the Newhouse Communications Center.

Curfews were strict. Fire alarms after curfew made it possible for the dorm supervisor to check for girls who were still not back. Although a loud ringing metal alarm was above my bed, I didn't hear it go off one Saturday night. The call went out that Marilyn was AWOL. When I was finally located sound asleep, the incident became a humorous joke among the students.

The stairs, coupled with the excitement of college and my normal high metabolism, caused my already thin frame to lose ten pounds in the first two weeks.

The doctor ordered me to have malted milk drinks, desserts and high-calorie food until my weight stabilized. While others were envious, they were not my favorite foods.

The most direct route to my class every morning was eighty-eight steps up a hill to Crouse College, home to the College of Visual and Performing Arts. It was a Romanesque revival building with gables, dormer windows and rounded arches. Inside was a huge mid-twentieth century pipe organ, chimes and bell tower. Carved hardwood designs representative of the period and stained glass windows were displayed throughout the building. Climbing the stairs to class was an awesome experience during the first few weeks.

One of the first art studio classes was figure drawing. An incredibly obese lady with rolls of flesh and dyed red hair took off her clothes, and we were told to draw her nude on our large pads. Mr. Houck, the professor in horned-rimmed glasses, said, "Drawing is a form of movement, so let your hands flow. If you draw the large concept first, the details will follow."

Syracuse University's picturesque main campus reflected its rich heritage, with an architectural mix of classic and contemporary academic buildings. The Hall of Languages and its early hillside companion, Crouse College, are listed in the National Register of Historic Places. The heart of the campus is its sweeping Quad, an open expanse of lawn and walkways, and a popular gathering place for students throughout the day. The autumn brings a fantastic array of colors, and in the winters, it is frequently covered in snow.

The assigned freshman roommate seemed like a nice, small-town girl from a suburb. She talked with an upstate accent, saying "rote," "kar," "merilyn," etc. Her teasing of my occasional New York City accent promptly eliminated my mixing up the "er" and "a."

Around holiday vacations, everyone on the floor except me started missing clothes. I assumed it was because they had the designer labels. Toward the end of the spring semester, my roommate was caught with the stolen items in her suitcase. Apparently, she "just did it for excitement" and was our resident kleptomaniac. She didn't need the clothes or money. It is weird how twisted people can become. At the end of her junior year, she married, became an Army wife, and was not missed.

Greek sorority and fraternity life were popular. At first, I didn't see much purpose in sororities, but later I saw how they could provide a family away from home and an enhanced social life. The sorority I eventually joined was housed in an attractive three-story stately home on Comstock Avenue and Marshall Street. Comstock was a tree-lined street and center mall surrounded by large three to four-story homes. Marshall Street contained the typical college shops and bars.

While Syracuse was a dry campus, a small use of beer by fraternities was overlooked. Large parties were supposed to be registered with the school, and hard alcohol was not permitted. Beer was sometimes allowed if there were responsible adult party supervisors. Students developed pre-party drinking blasts that circumvented the regulation. Attendees would be blindfolded and driven in a bus to an unknown designated area to drink the "rot gut" punch and get high before the social function. While transportation was provided and no one was forced to drink, two allotted drinks at the party instead might have avoided a lot of drunk, sick students.

Sorority pledging started that spring. While not in my original plan, becoming friends with some members changed my mind. In retrospect, the members found me. It was called "Sorority Rush" because members went out looking for potential pledges. Many sororities were look-alikes, but I valued individuality, so the group I joined comprised many diverse personalities.

Creature comforts were also a significant attraction. Their house had three floors of comfortable living accommodations, plus a cook and hired houseboys for serving food and odd jobs. The lifestyle was lavish compared to dorms, so I pledged and moved in. Life there included house rules such as standing for the Housemother when she walked into the room. The rules attempted to teach us to act like proper young ladies. Self-governance committees and changing roommates every semester were social ways of making new friends.

I found an unused side room in the basement and set it up as an art studio. Housemates were welcoming. Bridge games were always around to join, and they were willing to teach novices. The usual sorority and fraternity parties, panty raids, parade floats, formal dances, and activities typical of the 60s filled many fun times. I loved to dance and still treasure my "Twist Champ" trophy. When the Beatles entered the American scene, the group was an immediate hit and our favorite pop-culture group.

My first Thanksgiving ride home was in a 1929 Model T Ford, owned by a friend's brother. Foot to the pedal, top speed was 35 miles per hour—slower going uphill. He took passengers to Long Island for gas money. A deer froze in the headlights on our return to school. We tried to creep past him, but he ran out in front of the car at the last minute, hitting our fender. The guys jumped out to kill the deer and prevent suffering, but it couldn't be found. Thankfully, our damaged car still operated.

Mom had changed dramatically. She slowed down so much she could hardly walk across the room. Although only in her late 50s, she acted like a very old lady. Her children were gone, and her life purpose seemed finished; depression had set in again. Her predicament added more fuel to my fire for life beyond homemaking. I tried to give pep talks by phone and letters from school. Mom knew she needed to do something motivating outside of the house, so decided to attend classes for a real estate career. It pulled her out of the depression and gave her purpose for years to follow.

Sophomore year, I bleached my hair from ash blond to platinum blond with a home product and joined the official University Goon Squad pep committee. Jumping up and down leading crowd cheers at all the football games was energizing fun. However, a valuable lesson about networking was learned at the end of the year.

Twelve squad members were selected for Traditions, the Goon Squad's supervisory committee. Applicants had to write a paper about their plans and ideas for review and selection by the group. I was told by the one person I knew on the committee that while my application was full of inventive ideas and the acknowledged best presentation paper, I had lost because the committee didn't know me.

Who you know in life is very important. Being staunchly independent and not using connections is a sure way to get passed by. My "little sister" in the sorority made Traditions the following year, learning from my experience and utilizing several suggestions for some proposed campus activities and networking.

It never occurred to me to take an elective business course, so I learned by trial and error after completing school. In later years, I met a Harvard Business grad who admired my success. When I complained that I could have done better with a business school education, he replied, "I never did anything with my education. It takes motivation and ideas."

Historically, many family businesses have operated on the apprentice principle. In today's world, you don't have to have a degree to run a small business, although it helps. There are many practical online courses, certificates and degree programs. Marketing, venture capital, leadership, negotiation, and accounting are essential tools to understand. Classes can speed up the growth process, help avoid mistakes, and open your eyes to new thinking. With or without classes, owning a business will take work and perseverance.

My curiosity about the world was growing. I saw an opportunity to advance my general knowledge when a new Humanities Summer Program became available. The additional seven-credit course had classes for two weeks at both the beginning and end of summer. Between the bookended weeks of classes, the students read thirty books and wrote a paper. I read voraciously on the subway while commuting to my summer job, and whenever there was a moment.

The course investigated the human experience by reading from the classics of literature and philosophy. It was preceded and followed by weeks of small captivating discussion groups led by luminous professors.

The readings and discussions opened up many questions, leaving me feeling confused and restless. I had been naively optimistic about the world, but now the devastating events of history, man's inhumanity to man and the cruelties resulting from the need to survive weighed on my mind. American society seemed phony and shallow.

Knowing that I had just scratched the surface, I was ready to see more of the world. Syracuse University had a Semester-In- Italy Program that accepted sixty student applications. Open spaces were available to students from Syracuse and other universities.

My father's response to my request for the semester in Europe was, "Why go to Europe? Everyone comes to New York." He didn't enjoy travel, and his idea of touring a city was to walk from one end of the main street to the other—and leave. Perusing shops or stopping to eat in a quaint place cost money and was not his way of entertaining unless pressed.

Dad reluctantly signed the trip application because I told him it was unlikely the liberal arts program would accept an art student, and I agreed to pay any extra costs after graduation. More to his surprise than mine, I was accepted.

The ship's departure was scheduled for February of 1963. I was happy to learn that Judy, a sorority sister, and Ann, a girl from my freshman dorm, were part of the group.

That summer, I worked tedious jobs in a Manhattan accounting office while reading the course literature of Moliére, Thoreau and Voltaire on the train.

Much of the office work was adding numerous columns of numbers with a manual adding machine—producing rolls of paper on the floor. One job was typing checks—where every mistake was a "void." It was boring work.

My mind wandered to travel fantasies of Italy. Dreams of seeing the world would soon be coming true. I was excited about the pending European adventure and impatient for it to begin.

Chapter 7

World View

My parents looked worried, but wished me well as I jubilantly boarded the cruise ship. Finally, the departure time for my exciting ocean voyage arrived. The *Constitution*, a very prestigious ocean-liner in 1963, left from a Manhattan port on a cold, exhilarating day in February. The sixty students aboard this eleven-day cruise lived in lower-level steerage, but were allowed access to first-class facilities and events. We ate fantastic meals, watched the shows and played shuffleboard. Language classes were held daily. It was imperative that we learn to speak Italian as quickly as possible, because we would be living with a family where English was not understood. Every day we crammed lists of Italian vocabulary.

Our first glimpse of Europe revealed a delightful view of native boys in boats bringing flowers and jumping for coins at dawn. We had arrived at Madeira, a charming island off the coast of Portugal. As we later wandered through the picturesque town, the villagers charmed us with their warm smiles and friendly attitude. They had so little but knew how to spread happiness in a genuine way. Friendly natives gave the tourists local blooms and tried to sell whatever they could to the Americans for coins.

Our next port was Gibraltar, a British territory off the northern coast of Africa, with a view of two continents and two bodies of water. An entertaining taxi driver kept us laughing while providing a personal guided tour for a little more than the travel fare. As the owner of the local junkyard, he knew many people and entertaining anecdotes. While we drove around town, he articulated the colorful stories in a charming British accent, while pointing to the local attractions. He had a good sense of humor and told many jokes. The Gibraltar monkeys were everywhere and jumped on our backpacks to steal food and shiny objects.

Proceeding north up the coast of Italy, we stopped first at the densely-populated Italian city of Naples. Naples was an urban jungle with a tangled mass of people, scooters and cars. It was a lovable chaos of sidewalk living with no yards or balconies. Ship passengers could wander through the crowded, old city for the day, tour museums or visit the volcanic ruins of Pompeii. A few classmates and I opted for the side trip to Pompeii. We glimpsed ancient Roman life frozen in time by the eruption of Mt. Vesuvius. It was overpowering standing on these ruins of bygone times. History was no longer just dry pages in a textbook but alive in a way that we could touch.

Cruise ships are full of entertainment but can hit unwanted stormy seas. Back on the sea that night, the weather became turbulent. In the morning, my cabin mates were all seasick. I was okay, so I retrieved the medications from their suitcases and then went upstairs for breakfast, eagerly looking forward to the ship's meal. However, a full breakfast that day was not a wise idea. The walls started swaying, and I became nauseous when returning to my lower cabin. Running upstairs and staring out at the horizon line stabilized my stomach, so I didn't get sick, but wouldn't do that again.

Our boat's next and final cruise stop was the city of Genoa, Italy. A bus drove us from there through the breathtakingly picturesque Tuscany scenery of rolling green hills dotted with charming towns. Everyone was excited as we approached Florence, where we would meet our Italian host families. Sheila, a pretty blond with a hilarious sense of humor, was scheduled as my roommate for the first half of the semester. In the second half, we would switch to a new family and be on our own.

"Ciao," greeted Carla as our bus doors opened and we were led to our waiting hosts. Sheila nodded her head understandingly and said, "Si," to our signora's very fast Italian questions. I was amazed how Sheila had learned so much Italian on the ship, but it soon became evident she didn't understand a word! Luckily, Italians have a lot of patience with anyone trying to learn their language. Sheila's antics often had us laughing.

Carla was a single mother with two sons living away at a boarding school. She supported herself and her sons by taking in students. A Swiss and French girl were also living there when we arrived.

Carla explained that her husband had left her for another woman, so she had to take in students. She sadly told us that she didn't have any option for love again and was trapped. It was acceptable behavior for men to have affairs outside of marriage, but women could be easily disgraced. Divorce was not an option for a Roman Catholic wife, and she would be considered a fallen woman if she dared to have a romance. I was moved by her struggle, concluding her husband and the apparent double standard were heartless.

Carla, an attractive woman in her mid-thirties, demonstrated sensitivity and melodrama when she spoke. She could bubble with excitement and then sink into a dramatic cascade of tears, moaning that her life was over. It would be followed by a burst of laughter and hugs if you tried to make her happy. Carla said students were her only entertainment, so we loved to entertain her, and she lived vicariously through our stories. She was a lesson to me about how to laugh at the human plight and seize the day.

Sheila and I double-dated two Italians who were friends. Fabrizio was my beau, and Sheila dated Guido. Fabrizio told me that if a man began to date a local girl, they were always chaperoned. Families considered it a serious matter, so single men preferred to date Americans. Even though we were tourists with no family connections, they still feared the custom of coming to the girl's house for a date. To do so would mean a marriage proposal. We always had to meet outside on the street corner or at the theater. Fabrizio was my first introduction to a Communist. We had some fascinating conversations, and he had endless patience with my language mistakes. On one occasion he took me on a day trip with some friends to a ski mountain. I fell every few turns all the way down the mountain, but had a wonderful time.

While I loved the warmth of the Italian people, I realized America would always be my home. From what I could see, this charming Italian world had too many obstacles for women. Women were very overprotected. I thought it was outrageous that women were considered too easily influenced to be trusted alone with men. I felt it would suffocate my spirit.

My second family was the only Jewish family in the program. The Dean of Students didn't look at my record and thought it would be a unique experience for me. I looked like a small-town girl from the mid-west. Having grown up in a Jewish neighborhood, Italian Catholics were more uncommon. The members of this particular family were terrible cooks, a poor example of Jewish cooking. Their coffee was burnt grounds left on the stove for days, and the food was uninteresting. One night, they tried to serve me calf's brains for dinner. I had taken a squishy bite before asking—and then felt sick when I finally understood their sign language. Carla's fun personality and cooking were definitely preferred.

We had to boil water every morning for washing and were allowed only one bath a week, at both locations. The central heating was inadequate, so would dress quickly in the sunlight for warmth. I wore my winter coat every day to the dining room table throughout February and March.

We were in the epicenter of the Italian Renaissance, where people transitioned from the Middle Ages into an artistic explosion. I was wowed when I saw the original art of Michelangelo, Leonardo da Vinci, and Donatello. The colorful, often life-size originals were infinitely different from the small, black and white photos I had seen in my textbooks.

Immersed so entirely in a world of artistic genius and Italian culture, I wondered about the origins of creativity. Drifting off to sleep at night, I would often see images that had no relationship to my life and speculated that skillful artistic talent must see those images more consistently to paint them.

Biking and walking around town were our modes of transportation. Classrooms were at the Piazza Savonarola, named in honor of a Renaissance monk who was hanged and burned for reform teachings that angered the Catholic Church and the ruling Medici family.

My curriculum included seven credits of Italian, Opera & Society, and Art History. Studying for the Art History slide identification exam included memorizing every piece of art on the walls in museums around Florence. Only parts of a painting might be shown on a slide screen, and we would have to identify the artist from whatever piece was displayed. The Opera & Society class didn't provide translations for the libretto. We were expected to pick up the story from the performance of the music and our limited Italian vocabulary—a difficult task. I was stirred by how passionate the Italians felt about opera; they would scream "bravo" exhaustively.

At Easter, I traveled by train with Sheila and two other student friends, Judy and Diane, to Rome for the weekend. The modest Rome hotel felt like luxury living. We were thrilled to have hot, running water and heat at the hotel, no longer taking simple things for granted.

Rome was a glorious city, filled with ancient ruins, Vatican history, beautiful art, and vibrant people. We wandered around the city's attractions on Saturday, threw pennies in the Trevi Fountain and relaxed on the Spanish Steps. Easter Sunday, we joined the thousands of people in St. Peter's Square to see the Pope say

Mass. It was a short weekend trip, but we were hooked on the vast array of things to do and see. We all wanted to return.

It's so easy to fall in love with Italy—from the rolling hills of vineyards and olive groves to the busy streets of Florence with pedestrians strolling and chatting near the Duomo. Open markets sold everything from fresh vegetables to leather coats. The Ponte Vecchio, a historic downtown bridge in Florence, displayed many exclusive jewelry stores in the pricy shopping area.

Bargaining with shopkeepers was standard for Italians, but not the tourists. Becoming comfortable with negotiating prices was a skill later utilized in business. I learned to walk away if I couldn't get my price. They would always come back with a compromise.

Traffic lights were rare, so motorcyclists would zoom past in all directions, and one quickly became street savvy. We were surprised not to see a pizza stand. There was only one small store where pizza could be purchased, so it was more an American treat than Italian in 1963. My favorite side trip was the very romantic Fiesole. We would watch the magic of the sunset over Florence from this charming ancient Etruscan city, nestled above on a hillside of olives and cypresses.

After the four-month semester, I had a fair conversational ability in Italian. Since I was told that the liberal arts credits might not transfer as BFA requirements for graduation, I focused more on speaking than on using perfect grammar. When in conversations with my boyfriend, Fabrizio, I could communicate faster without all the ideal endings on verbs. Speaking primarily in only four tenses—past, present, future and imperfect— the conversation was quicker on general subjects—enough to make myself understood.

Diane and I planned a summer tour of Europe together. She was a straight "A" student in Italian and spoke with correct grammar. However, I did most of the Italian communication because I could get it out fast in four tenses. Diane's knowledge of German was very helpful when we reached Germany and Switzerland.

Our guidebook was "Europe on $5 a Day" by Arthur Frommer. A two-month Eurail Train Pass provided unlimited travel between Italy, France, Switzerland, Germany, Holland, Sweden, Denmark, Norway and England.

We sometimes used the train as an overnight hotel or stayed in hostels to save money. The train compartment was composed of two facing seats that slid down into one large double bed at night. We would pretend to go to sleep early and draw the shades, hoping no one would come into the compartment, but it didn't always work. People might just pile in during the middle of the night. One night, there were five people sleeping in one bed. This included a soldier, a mother and her small child, Diane and me. Another time on a crowded train, I slept sitting on a suitcase, propped up against a wall because all the compartments were full. In those days I could sleep through most anything. Fellow passengers were respectful and colorful companions, often telling us their stories, if we could communicate through the language differences.

Each country had a unique personality. Many of the stereotypes that I had dismissed as fictitious came to life. Soldiers marched in the Germany train station. The precise Germans wouldn't let us leave our hostel room in the morning until the bed was made with perfect hospital corners and no wrinkles. The cunning French tried to charm us while cheating us out of money, then laughed when we caught them.

Numerous small adventures diverted us from common tourist routes. In Venice, we met two attractive American guys who had been pick-pocketed by one of the local thieves. This led to a ride on a police motorboat attempting to locate the suspects.

Two strange men followed us through a dark park on our way to a youth hostel in Germany. The hostel turned out to be closed, and going back the same way through the park seemed very risky. Some nearby stairs led down to an unknown destination. We took them. Below, we found ourselves next to the rushing Rhone River with the city high above on the cliffs. The two men continued to follow us and were closing in. As we walked faster, they walked faster. Not knowing what to do, we decided to take our chances with a strange man walking ahead alone. Luckily, he understood our broken German and sign language. He showed us the best path back to the busy central city.

In Chamonix, France, we took a breathtaking cable car to the snowy peak at Mont Blanc and back. I might not have taken the ride, if I had known the frightening heights. Copenhagen offered a boat docked in the harbor as a unique youth hostel. At the Stockholm train station, we were pleasantly surprised to find that the friendly Swedes opened up family homes to visitors, so tourists could book a home for the night in a similar manner to a hotel.

Diane flew back the United States at the end of our eight weeks, and I made the cheaper voyage home on a studentship named *The Groote Beer*. It was a rickety old boat filled with students trying to save money. We were told the ship was on its last voyage halfway across the ocean. We hoped it wouldn't sink.

At dinner the first night on the ship, I sat at a long table next to Ashok Dar, a Fulbright scholar from India on his way to Cornell University. We had a fascinating discussion during which he mentioned that palm reading had been in his family for centuries. I jokingly asked him to read my palm. He refused, saying he didn't read palms much anymore. The next night I asked him again, and he still hedged.

On the third night, he looked quickly at my palm and suggested a meeting in the lounge at an appointed time. I arrived—not knowing what to expect. Even in my youth, my palm was filled with many small lines, like an old lady's hand. For a captivating two hours he explained aspects of my personality and described the future. He also told how to read the lines.

"Palm reading cannot tell specific events, but can only tell probabilities and age brackets. Over time, signs can change, with small lines affecting the outcome and new lines appearing. A triangle means that the event would be controlled by the person's own skill, a box means general protection, and a star good fortune. The hand most used is the forecast path, and the other hand is our nature." He added a lot more details, and several times he warned against using what he taught. "Lines can change, so it is dangerous to make predictions, especially if negative."

There is a scientific basis in palm reading. Except for the brain, the fingers possess twenty times more concentrated sensory nerve endings than any other part of our body. There are a total of about 17,000 touch receptors and nerve endings. Each fingerprint is unique and can be used for identification. Our genes are powerful messengers, and twins separated at birth will often travel the same pattern into parallel lives. Probability patterns for the future could have been chronicled in the lines. Ashok warned that there are many frauds. People exaggerate and dramatize to make money, thereby creating tales about the future which are impossible to derive from a hand.

Ashok's predictions took on an inquisitive dimension throughout my life. Although I still attributed it to coincidences, I always wondered if destiny plays a part in our opportunities. Try as I might, I wasn't able to make some things happen.

He predicted that although I would soon meet my first love, it wouldn't last, and my marriage would be much later. My life line had conflict lines so my life wouldn't be easy, but I would succeed in most endeavors. There was a strong, successful career line splitting into two parts later in life. Many events, numerous flirtations, and "an interesting life" were to come. There was a probable late-life romance. He foretold quite a few children and said they might not all be my own. He added that one child would have serious problems, but the problems would fade with time. While I would be reasonably comfortable, great wealth would not be achieved. The main warning was to watch out for difficulties after age sixty. An ancient warning symbol of "death at sea" appeared on one mound. It was generally interpreted to mean just some severe problem. "Observe carefully near that age," he cautioned. "We can sometimes change our destiny, and protections can appear." I left the ship with a little knowledge of palm reading along with my supposed fate, while still thinking it was all unlikely to be true.

Back in the states, my new knowledge became a party game for a while. Then the predictions took an ominous turn. At a single's gathering in Manhattan, I met a guy in his early twenties and read his palm. Seeing only one short marriage line at a young age, I blurted out that I saw a very early marriage, which couldn't be true, or he wouldn't be at that singles party. He blanched. Tragically, his wife had been killed in a car crash the year before. I could see by his expression that my words confirmed his determination never to marry again. I ceased the potentially dangerous party game.

The following October, I met an appealing guy with an adventuresome spirit who touched my young heart. After our first date, I woke up the next morning and felt very different. For the first time, an all-enveloping sensation surged through my body and consumed my mind. Of course, I was at the right age for a first love, so it would have been expected, but it was a new experience for me. My new amour had been in the military service before attending college, so he was a little older and, to me, more sophisticated. He too wanted an exciting life in New York City. At my vulnerable age of nineteen, his appearance and ambitions coincided with my desire to live in New York City for an unconventional life. After two dates, I became smitten. However, after Thanksgiving recess, he returned with a wedding ring on his hand. Birth control pills had just come on the market, but he had gotten a girlfriend at home pregnant. Our romance never got started.

Illusions can create as much pain as the real thing, so my young heart seemed broken. Of course, it was just wishful thinking and not a relationship of substance. Talking things out with others would have been a good release, but I held it all inside. Someone probably would have told me to fill my life with new activities to forget him, as most of my life lay before me with exciting adventures yet to come. Instead, I sulked, feeling my only chance had passed me by, fueled by self-pity. A couple of years later, I ran into him in Manhattan when he was job hunting, and I was an art director in an advertising agency. The magic had ended, and I wondered why I had wasted my time. It wasn't my last time falling for an illusion.

Graduation in 1964 was a celebration day, although it was also sad to leave my friends and comfort zone. The university had opened up a world of people and ideas that had begun to shape the bigger picture. I had changed my major from fashion illustration to advertising design and was excited about working in the Manhattan advertising world. I knew there was a lot ahead for me and was ready for whatever cards were dealt, still determined to play them the best that I could.

The previous year gave historical evidence to my yearnings for an independent life. Betty Freidan's book *The Feminine Mystique*, published in 1963, sparked the women's movement of the 60s. She argued that the suburbs were "burying women alive." It was an idea whose time had come for my generation. The world was moving to a different sound, and I was going to be part of the music.

Chapter 8

The Glass Ceiling

After graduation, I quickly found a job in an advertising agency's "Bull Pen," but postponed living in Manhattan until I had paid off debts to my father for European trip costs. I vowed never to live in debt again and hated my income going to past expenses instead of current interests. ~~Moreover,~~ I was stuck in sprawling suburbia again. It was depressing to be away from all my college friends and fun."

I lived for my job in Manhattan. However, standing on the long bus and train commute was tedious. During the crowded 45-minute train ride, men still frequently tried to rub against me. I was accosted almost daily by normal-looking businessmen, and always had to be alert to move out of their way.

My new job was at Grey Advertising, a global advertising and marketing agency headquartered in New York City. In 1964, billings reached $100 million. In 1965, the firm went public, and in 1966 it was one of the top ten agencies. It was a great place to start, even if my job was at the bottom.

The advertising agency job spec required a college degree and portfolio, but the only skills of genuine interest to them appeared to be my typing and office proficiencies. My official title was "Gal Friday." The Bull-Pen, or art studio, comprised mostly of men and a couple of women, produced printer-ready art, plus renderings and storyboards for presentations. In later years, the title would be called "Administrative Assistant" in the Art Studio.

I was quickly told not to aspire to become an art director, even though I had the same BFA degree as the men. Women became only art buyers. There were seventy men and no women in art director positions. The glass ceiling was apparent.

I stepped up to do whatever was needed when my two male bosses took time off to play. The Bull Pen's studio manager was a good-looking Italian named Andy who would go out on long martini lunches with his girlfriends, leaving me to run the department and assign the projects. The first time it happened was an accident. I stepped in when the desk wasn't covered, and all ran smoothly. Thereafter, the assignment desk was frequently left to me. It didn't go unnoticed by others.

There were no agencies to call for help. Frantic rushes to find people for a busy workload necessitated calling from a list. As the Gal Friday, one of my tasks was to telephone freelance talent. I made up an A-list, B-list and C-list, scored for skills and availability.

Wanting to move beyond my Gal Friday job, I enrolled in two reasonably-priced classes at the School of Visual Arts. One class was to improve my production skills, and the other was writing advertising headline concepts. I also volunteered to stay without pay for agency evening assignments.

Soon I was much more valuable than in my original position. The daughter of a major client was given to me as an assistant. Her wealthy family wanted to teach her a lesson about life. She had been married to a guy who wouldn't work and divorced with two children at nineteen. My new assistant was anxious to see a woman get an opportunity, so she cooperated fully with whatever I asked. She just casually threw her mink boa into the file cabinet and pitched right in.

At eight months, the head creative director offered me a promotion to become an Art Director in his creative group. The glass ceiling was broken.

A few nice guys asked me out to lunch, and several married men made passes. The viable guys were looking for wives who would live in suburbia with their children, immediately evaporating any possible appeal. I had no interest in suburban living or in married men.

Looking for some social life during that first year, I made trips into Manhattan with Jeanie. We explored the singles scene on weekends and found a sociable "Happy Hour" at Fridays' Restaurant & Bar on East 69th Street. We were among the first single women to populate it before it became a larger franchise. In the summer, our destination was Manasquan on the Jersey shore, a popular beach resort full of young singles. The crowd would dance on the beach during the day and party in the Osprey Bar at Happy Hour. Jeanie christened me with the new nickname, "Buckets," perhaps because I was not a heavy drinker or endowed with what men might call buckets. Maybe it meant I would make buckets of money.

After my debts were paid, my parents expected me to pay rent and live at home until I married. I said, "No thanks." It was time to live my life. Dad had always wanted a home where he could live, so he couldn't understand why I wanted to move. He actually had a tear in his eye as I left. I was jubilant and told him not to worry.

Jeanie drove me in her convertible to the Barbizon Hotel for Women in midtown Manhattan. She was about to leave on her own adventure of a job transfer to ground stewardess in California. Jeanie looked like a "California Girl" and now would be one. The surfer lifestyle was planned for her time off.

Manhattan life felt charged with opportunities and excitement. My twenties became full of friends, parties, travel cross-country, ski houses and more.

Linda, an attractive blond from Manhasset on Long Island was living at the Barbizon, and also looking for a roommate. We signed a one-year sublease for a large single-bedroom apartment in a modern building on East 70th Street. Her Assistant Buyer discount at J.C. Penny helped with the cost of setting up our apartment.

Neither of us had any idea how to cook. We even had to read the instructions on a frozen corn package. Our first cookbook was *The Can Opener's Cookbook*. We progressed to *The Joy of Cooking* and other cookbooks, eventually entertaining with delicious dinner parties.

Linda loved her job, and her intention was to become a career woman. She never wanted to get married and feared childbirth. As fate would have it, she fell in love with her boss and was the first one of us to tie the knot two years later. Her marriage has lasted over thirty years, with two children. Never say "never," and always expect the unexpected.

A number of Linda's friends from Manhasset were already living in the city and became my friends as well. Joan was a 5'10" attractive natural blond of Norwegian descent who did administrative work at *Time-Life*. Mary Lou had a terrific sense of humor and sharp wit, which often had us in tears with laughter. The third, Louise, a more laid-back French major, had a brother who frequently joined our outings.

Linda and I later added a third roommate to our single-bedroom apartment. Liz was raised by a ski instructor family near Bromley Mountain, Vermont. Since I had winter vacation time to use, she suggested staying with her family at a nominal fee and sign up for a learn-to-ski week. I could ride back and forth to the mountain with her father. My only previous experience skiing was in northern Italy with Fabrizio and it had been enormous fun. I jumped at the opportunity. Her friendly father and mother were classic native Vermonters. They lived in a heated log cabin and both smoked corn-cob pipes.

My very handsome ski instructor added to the attraction and exhilaration of skiing. He excitedly described his adventures of skiing while working at resorts and encouraged a winter out west to learn the sport. The idea was intriguing.

Manhattan residents frequently traveled for weekend and vacation entertainment to get-a-way retreat houses near beaches or in the mountains. Singles often joined group houses, which provided companionship and a well-priced escape from the hot summer cement.

Fire Island and several eastern Long Island towns, generally referred to as the Hamptons, were the most popular places for the singles scene. Fire Island attracted a casual Manhattan crowd for spontaneous, relaxing weekends. It contained a number of different communities off the southern coast of Long Island. Stores and roads didn't exist in many areas, so all the food had to be brought over from the mainland on the commuter boat.

The Hamptons had a different vibe. Magnificently designed estates with manicured lawns and strategically perched mansions near dunes attracted many from the Upper Eastside and Wall Street. The weekends from both Fire Island and the Hamptons ended with a long, slow ride back on Sunday nights amid bumper-to-bumper traffic on the Long Island Expressway.

During our first summer, Louise, Mary Lou and Louise's brother signed up for about four weekends at a group house in The Pines on Fire Island. They didn't know much about The Pines but quickly found out that it was a homosexual community. The community was comprised of mostly men, but included some lesbians and straights. In order to have some compatible company, they invited straight friends as guests for a fun weekend at the beach. Beyond the ocean views of beautiful sandy beaches and scattered houses with dinner parties, the main group attraction was a large dance hall near the water. Everyone danced around the room, moving from group to group and from partner to partner.

A friend from high school came up to me in the dance hall, but I didn't recognize him at first. Barry had become a 1960s love child with long hair and love-beads. We stayed in touch over the years through many coincidental meetings on Manhattan buses or walking along the street, so it seemed like he had a purpose in my life. At the encounter on the Pines dance floor, we both gasped in surprise at each other, "What are you doing here?" The pregnant pause seemed to imply we were both a part of the homosexual community, but we just smiled at each other and continued dancing. I learned in later years that Barry died in his forties, a victim of the awful AIDS disease.

As we were finishing dinner at our group house that night, two guys started making-out with each other at the table, then continued on the couch. After the initial shock was over, I was curious to understand more. The following morning, I had a long talk with the` tall dark haired guy. He was married but often spent weekends at The Pines because he "liked variety." He professed to also love his wife. The way he said it seemed reasonable but sad. In my view, he didn't love deeply and seemed only capable of shallow relationships.

The second year, I took a partial share at Davis Park with Mary Lou, Louise and her brother. It was a straight community, but still without stores or cars. The atmosphere was congenial with nightly gatherings. At 6 p.m. many from the town would congregate for a "sixish" at the water's edge, bringing their cocktails for socializing until sunset.

Back at my office on Monday mornings, fellow employees would sometimes be missing. Pink dismissal slips were routinely handed out on Fridays with the paychecks, and the fired employees would not return. Grey Advertising had a reputation at that time for its revolving door policy. I survived the purges because I was paid low, attractive to some of the men, capable of drawing storyboards and efficient at getting deadline-driven projects completed by my friends in the Bull Pen.

I stood aghast when some senior account managers acted like nasty drill sergeants, denigrating and ripping into their subordinate junior account executives as a display of authority. While a stern method of keeping men in line might sometimes be needed, this male hazing method of just exerting power was, in my opinion, unnecessary. It seemed verbally and psychologically abusive to pleasant young men who did nothing to deserve it. The guys accepted the hazing as just part of business, but I didn't. While my immediate bosses were pleasant, I didn't agree with these male tactics and could never run a business that way.

TV commercials are created by a copywriter and art director team. The presentation before the account management group required a sales concept and script, plus preparation of a finished storyboard. Sometimes there would be a week to work on it, but it was common policy to just allow a matter of hours. Quality work required thought and discussions, preferably allowing at least one overnight. It was hard to feel conviction when given only three hours.

The meeting of critics was the worst part. My writer would usually put lines into the script for the assembled group to change—hoping that the basic ideas wouldn't get destroyed. After we presented the idea and gave a sales pitch, the conference room of men would try to pick it apart and find fault. Every junior and senior account executive wanted to justify his job by making a correction. I had always hated getting up in front of groups, and this situation couldn't have been worse. I felt frustrated and blocked.

As an added hurdle, the senior producer and his team tried to usurp the credits for my commercial by stampeding over my instructions. A general rivalry exists with some producers who want to be thought of as part of the creative imprint. When I received a follow-up assignment for an award-winning commercial on the *Ideal Toys* account, the producer saw me as easy prey, ignored what I wanted to be done, and instructed the crew otherwise.

Male art directors could keep the thundering herd at bay but I wasn't tough enough to tame that group of bulls. While everyone realized the diminished result of the campaign was the producer's fault, I was very young and it was evident that I didn't know how to play in the men's game. Everyone expected me to be competent without training or help. The rule was sink or swim.

Chapter 9

The Call

During my time working at Grey Advertising, equal pay and equal offices did not exist. When I asked for a raise, I was told the men needed more money and prestige than women, so my raise could not match their salaries. Everyone kept telling me women didn't really need to make money. The office politics didn't fit my aspirations, and I knew I would always be swimming upstream. The writing was on the wall. My inner voice said to quit and have some fun. I had played the cards dealt the best I could for two years but was thwarted, so it was time for a new adventure.

I've learned that risk-taking is a necessary part of entrepreneurship. Some people suggest first jumping out of a plane in a parachute before going into business for oneself. That wouldn't have been my suggestion. However, stepping out of the comfort zone and risk-taking can eventually lead to opportunity. An adventuresome spirit is needed. Entrepreneurship requires taking well-researched chances, a unique combination of skills that might be considered an oxymoron. Starting up any new business requires both research and risk. Later, I would have to carefully make risky decisions for to my business.

My inner guide didn't hesitate when the converging events pointed to a new adventure. Learning to ski out West while working for an inn or restaurant sounded like a fun way to travel on a budget. Our Manhattan apartment lease was ending the following fall, making it a perfect time to move on. I told my employer and family six months in advance that I would be quitting the following fall to go skiing. Neither my family nor employer believed me, doubting that I would really abandon such a prestigious job as art director. Dad reacted by saying, "You can't run away from your problems."

I answered, "I'm not running away. I'm running toward something that is calling me." A skiing adventure created intoxicating music to my ears, summoning me to the next phase. The new hand of cards had been dealt.

Working at a ski resort in exchange for a room and lift pass would be a fun way to travel and learn to ski. Others didn't see it the same way, but I needed to find my place in the world. This adventure felt like a growth opportunity.

I mailed letters inquiring about employment in Aspen, Colorado, and Alta, Utah. Replies arrived several weeks later with, "Lots of jobs. Come on out."

Joan decided to join me. Her administrative job at *Time Inc.* had become boring, so she was ready for something new. Linda planned to move into her apartment spot when she left. Then, while at a party, we both met Roz, a pretty model who was the great-great-granddaughter of Nathaniel Hawthorne. She was heading to Denver to meet up with her doctor fiancée.

Together we signed up with an auto-drive service, driving someone else's car cross-country. Two weeks before we departed, Mary Lou left a note under my door: "I quit my job today and am joining you."

At the beginning of November, the four of us loaded a gleaming new Buick to its limit and set out to visit some friends on our way to Aspen. The owners would have been chagrined to see the luggage rack on top and the car loaded heavily for four women. We washed and vacuumed later, so they never realized it went through rain and snow while overloaded with baggage. Fortunately, there were no damages.

The cross-country trip to Aspen was a high-spirited adventure filled with hilarity and camaraderie. Mary Lou, our trip comedian, kept us entertained with funny stories and her imitations of the locals. Roz provided a lot of material for Mary Lou's jokes—as she was always preoccupied with her makeup and clothes, never getting out of her high heels. In St. Louis, Missouri, Columbus, Ohio, and Denver, Colorado, we had relatives who provided free lodging and entertainment.

As we reached Colorado, the stunning Rocky Mountains loomed up from the flat plains in the distance. They were breathtaking and beautiful. Roz had such an enjoyable time on the trip that she decided to postpone joining her fiancée in Denver and instead went on with us to Aspen.

Aspen greeted us with an early November snow. Jobs were not as easy as implied by the letters, as returning regulars took most of them. I stopped by one of the two local newspapers, the *Aspen Illustrated News*. They quickly jumped at the good fortune of having a New York art director work for them. The paper had its rush time toward the end of the day, to print early morning. The proposed starting schedule at three p.m. fit my skier hours. The salary was minimum wage plus a ski pass. Most of the work was boring, but I illustrated a few ads and front pages.

After knocking on many doors, Joan and Mary Lou found waitress jobs with housing. All seasonal jobs included a ski pass, and some jobs added food or low-rent housing.

After a month, Roz returned to her fiancé. Her high heels and make-up didn't fit the rugged lifestyle, and she disliked skiing. Mary Lou initially hated skiing, but a ski instructor romance changed that. Her skill soon surpassed the rest of us who couldn't afford lessons.

The aim was to ski all day, then work late afternoons and nights. My newspaper job gradually increased in hours without an increase in pay. The supervisor knew I was unsatisfied but wouldn't accommodate my request. On New Year's Eve day, a chairlift acquaintance told me she was leaving her job, and I could have it. I immediately quit the newspaper to work as a "salad girl" at the beautiful Crystal Palace.

The Crystal Palace, an impressive, lively, well-known restaurant and nightspot, was in a glorious old building. Stained glass windows adorned three-quarters of the red velvet wall. Elegant chandeliers hung from the ceiling. All the waitresses and waiters were actresses and actors who sang Broadway show tunes from the aisles between courses. Every night this restaurant was filled with energy and superb performances.

Staff was fed the same food as the patrons in a sit-down dinner before the show began, a delicious perk.

The kitchen staff prepared a couple of hundred dinners for each of the two shifts. I was able to watch the show from the kitchen door, and the music drifted into our work area.

The job required making all the appetizers, salads and desserts at break-neck speed. Lettuce heads were cleaned and stored in standard clean garbage bins lined with large plastic bags and then served up into salads. It was intense work—with rarely a break from four p.m. until midnight. If I worked really fast, I could see more of the show.

I soon realized that as the only woman in the kitchen, I was expected to work harder than the men. Two guys of my same rank teased how they had it so much easier. One night, the chef wanted me to stay after hours to do extra chores but said the guys could go home. I had a date and said I had to leave, suggesting he ask the guys instead. Feeling girls were controllable, he threatened to fire me if I walked out the door. Since this was just an adventure and I had savings, I called his bluff and walked out.

The club's owner approached me on the ski slope the next day to talk. He arbitrated the dispute and asked me to return. The guys got more work after that incident.

The skiing was fantastic, and my skill gradually improved. It is the only sport I ever really loved. Going down the mountain's picturesque landscape to the rhythm of my skies was exhilarating.

Ajax was the closest mountain to town but had only expert trails. Snowmass, a newly-developed mountain for beginners, seemed too easy for our goals. Although starting as beginner skiers, my friends and I took season passes for the Aspen Highlands, an intermediate to advanced skill mountain. The chair lift traveled over a very steep precipice before reaching the peak, often stopping in the middle, leaving everyone dangling at a scary height. Then, a narrow path with steep side drops had to be navigated as a skier went from the lift to the main slope—definitely not a place to "crash and burn."

The mountain was not for the faint of heart. These were considerably taller mountains than what I had seen in Italy or Vermont. Determined not to let my fear of heights spoil the adventure, I pushed forward and overcame acrophobia, eventually feeling comfortable in the situation. The more you learn and are successful, the better you control fear.

When navigating huge moguls of snow early in the season, I took a nasty fall on my back. I didn't break anything, but it made me think twice about living dangerously. Maintaining control is critical to the completion of any successful adventure.

The "Après Ski" happy hour scene at numerous restaurants was always filled with flushed and cheerful skiers. Conversations centered around skiing and the weather. We often watched competitive races, including awesome ski jumping. Members of the ski patrol were our local buddies. The Aspen area was a year-round, scenic community lending itself well to other types of recreation, such as cross-country skiing and snowshoeing, fly-fishing and hiking.

I had my usual casual dates. A memorable one was a good-looking, sensitive guy named Oliver, whom I dated a few times until we drifted apart. Several months later, he committed suicide. I'm sure loneliness was a factor, but there was sadness in his eyes that I was never able to reach. The situation was more devastating than I realized. I reflected on him as a fragile soul who needed a deep loving relationship. It made me think about the vulnerability of life and how a broken spirit or broken heart can make life unbearable. I would do my best to not get sucked into that downhill depression spiral by keeping a positive attitude.

Of course, the Aspen ski-bum life was a very superficial existence to me. Only the here-and-now counted in our crowd of drifters, and no one had a past life. "Don't ask" about the person's past life was the unspoken rule. Unfortunate or criminal backgrounds might be uncovered. One night, the cops arrested an acquaintance, and he never returned. Drugs were suspected.

Thanks to Mary Lou, I'm confident that we were the only ski-bums in Aspen who had the *New York Times* delivered. She was an avid reader and always commented on world events. The local papers provided one column of world news once a week— believing most of the community was just interested in regional topics. Generally, conversations were about community happenings, weather, skis and bindings.

Before coming to Aspen, Mary Lou had applied for work at the FBI. They took two years to check her background for the customary security clearance. Toward the end of the winter, she was invited to an interview in Washington, D.C. Although not sure she still wanted to join the FBI, she took the free plane fare back East. At the interview she learned the position required her to drop out of sight for two years, so she declined and returned to New York. Joan stayed with me until the end of the season but then headed back as well.

As the ski season ended, I was still restless and not ready to return. Mexico, a popular off-season retreat for many ski bums, called to me. Three guy friends were heading there, so I joined Bill, Dexter and Ron. Bill was a friend of Joan's from home. We drove south in his old black Mercedes Benz to Mexico, first visiting a vast red rock canyon in Arizona and then entering through Nogales.

The first stop in Mexico was the bathroom. "Montezuma's Revenge" hit with a severe case of dysentery. Although previously warned not to drink the water, we forgot about the ice cubes. An English couple staying at our guesthouse in this small town just past the U.S. border suggested "Entero Viroformo," a medication banned in the U.S. but sold over the counter in Mexico. I took the pills before meals for a couple of weeks, then only one a day. It worked wonders! By the end of the month, I could eat from street vendors like a local.

The roads going south wound through miles of badlands with mounds of barren rock, scattered impoverished villages, and children begging for money. We stopped at Guadalajara, a sleepy but charming university town—nothing like it appears today. There were no shopping malls or tall buildings. We observed a local dating ceremony. All eligible boys and girls came to the town square to flirt while circling the center statue. The boys walked in one direction and the girls the opposite direction, hoping to find a potential mate.

The exciting capital, Mexico City, bustled with busy people, tall buildings and colorful museums. I was enthralled by the dramatic and vibrant Mexican artwork—in particular Diego Rivera. Captured by the environment, I purchased a small colorful example from a street vendor as a reminder. Outside the city, we climbed the towering pyramids of Teotihuacan, once the metropolis of a mysterious civilization before the Aztecs.

Our next stop was the famous resort town of Acapulco. Sleeping on the pristine white sand beaches in the resort town seemed like a good idea for a great price. We mentioned the idea to some new friends staying at Las Brisas, a fancy upscale hotel complex. They said we were welcome to use their shower when needed. It was a beautiful night with the town activity just across the main beach road. The first night went well. The second night a creep lay down next to me and I didn't notice. Fortunately, my companions awoke quickly and chased off the intruder.

After Acapulco, we traveled up the coast to the small but talked-about town of Zihuatanejo. We were tired and it was very quiet. Hammocks hung from trees on the beach and we put them to immediate use. During the night, crabs and creatures ran all over the sand beach and under our hammocks. We didn't dare put a foot down. It was so quiet that I thought, "What possibly could happen here and why is this town well known?" We found out.

During the night, men with machine guns pushed us awake. Frightened, we answered their questions in broken Spanish and sign language. The next day, we learned that they were a police patrol. Zihuatanejo was notorious for Timothy Leary and his drug shipments. Finally, acknowledging that beaches could be dangerous at night, we stayed in guesthouses thereafter.

Although the drug culture had begun to reach the East Coast, it was more prevalent in California, some western states and Mexico. Locals invited us to a dinner party and we were hungry. The lasagna and brownies were made with hash, and the crowd was stoned on at least marijuana. I was hungry and ate the food—waiting to feel the effect. Nothing happened. Neither my friends nor I were interested in the drug scene other than as a curiosity. I used my father's trick about cigarettes—just take it to your lips and don't inhale.

After over a month in Mexico, it was time to move on. The guys headed home or back to Aspen for the summer. I took the lowest-priced bus from Mexico to San Diego, California to visit a ski-patrol friend met in Aspen. My bus turned out to be filled with Mexican laborers and chickens in cages. I was the only English-speaking passenger.

Since I couldn't call my friend when the bus arrived in San Diego 1 a.m., I searched for a hotel near the station. The hotels with vacancy signs suddenly had no room available for me when I asked. Something seemed wrong. Exasperated, I pointedly demanded a reason and found out that I was presumed to be a hooker. After promising not to bring anyone into the hotel, I was given a room. Bolting the door with furniture, I slept soundly.

The next day, my friend arrived. We drove around San Diego, a small charming town back then. Amidst the attractions was a unique zoo where the animals roamed without cages. In years to come, many zoos were modeled after it, but it was the first cage-free zoo for me. After a fun couple of days, I bid goodbye while boarding a bus to Los Angeles. The next stop was a prearranged visit with Jeanie, my childhood friend who had moved to California.

Jeanie threw a curveball. I had anticipated a sightseeing tour in Los Angeles, including the famous movie star districts of Hollywood and Beverly Hills. Perhaps we would spend a day with the surfers near her home in Redondo Beach. However, upon arrival, Jeanie shocked me by announcing she was leaving for an abortion. Her boyfriend was driving her to a doctor in Mexico. I had walked into the middle of a sad situation—planned, it seemed, for my arrival.

The first day was spent alone in her apartment complex without a car, waiting for her return. Her boyfriend then left her in my care that evening. When Jeanie started hemorrhaging, I drove her to the hospital, where she received a D&C. We finally got to bed in the early morning hours. I learned her boyfriend's family objected to him marrying her.

She recovered, but it could have ended much more tragically. By the next night, she felt a little better, so we went for a short drive around Los Angeles without stopping anywhere. Our interests, social scenes, values and aspirations had taken different paths. We had grown apart, and I was glad to leave on a plane to Hawaii.

Many of my skier friends had told tales of Hawaii, so it sparked my curiosity and imagination.

Chapter 10

Aloha

Hawaiians, in local native dress and garlands of fresh flowers around their necks, greeted all new airport arrivals. They passed out fresh flower leis to the visitors. The smell from the flowers was a seducing introduction to an enchanting new culture. I wandered around the capital city of Waikiki on the large island of Oahu, observing the landscape and people. The massive mountains jutting out of the water, created by lava thrown high into the air by volcanoes, were immediately breathtaking. Some active volcanoes still exist on the island. Around the shore were white sandy beaches with emerald-blue water, surrounded by palm trees under tranquil blue skies.

Alone and knowing no one, I approached three girls around my age in muumuu dresses, sitting on the stone wall of a downtown garden. I asked if they knew where I could find a room to live for a few months. Fortuitously, they happened to be looking for a roommate. I moved into a pleasant place in an old building near the beach. As with most of the older buildings in Hawaii at that time, there was a severe cockroach problem. Turning on the light at night in the bathroom or kitchen yielded hundreds of roaches, running across everything, including toothbrushes. Wisely, the living area had wall-to-wall carpeting. The bugs didn't cross the carpet. Apparently, roaches were impossible to exterminate with what was available in the 1960s. Although disgusting, I learned to live with it, as the rent and roommates were enjoyable.

A cocktail waitress job had always seemed glamorous and exciting, so I started going on a job search by applying in person at restaurants. To secure a position, and assuming that I could learn quickly, I indicated experience in Aspen. A few days later, an emergency call came in from Henri Louie's Beach Walk Cafe, a steak, lobster and spaghetti restaurant one block from the Hilton. Their cocktail waitress had quit that day, and I was needed immediately to be the only waitress in a bustling cocktail lounge next to the restaurant.

It became evident that I didn't know what I was doing. All the drink orders had to be separated into their liquor types before calling them into the woman bartender in a specific order. It was an old system making it easy for the bartender but difficult for the waitress. From what I can determine, it doesn't exist anymore. When the drinks were ready, I had to garnish them with a flower or condiments and deliver the glasses back in the original order to the right customers. This takes some practice under any conditions. In Hawaii, there were many exotic drinks complicating the task. In addition to being slow, I put the wrong flowers on cocktails, pepper on a Brandy Alexander, and spilled a drink on some poor customer. I was sure I would get fired, but they were desperate for help. Just in time, I caught on and was asked back the next night. Once I got into the rhythm, all went smoothly, and I enjoyed the job and customers. Some nights I worked as the hostess for the restaurant section, which was more relaxing.

The days were spent sleeping on the beach before getting ready to work and party again in the evening. When the lounge closed, various groups would go out to socialize until breakfast. Some of the locals I met were very strange, but then the crowd I traveled with was mostly filled with drifters.

The restaurant's owner was a hugely obese Hawaiian man who always tried to pinch my rear if I got close. Sexual harassment was an expected norm, so I just tried to stay out of his way. A well-seasoned Hawaiian woman in her late thirties controlled the bar. She had a reputation for having stabbed an ice pick through a man's hand when he tried to grab her inappropriately. I learned quickly not to cross either of them.

My roommate's favorite entertainment was the Ouija Board. I wondered, "Could it really be talking to the spirits?" By the end of the summer and hundreds of sessions later, I concluded it was somehow reading my mind and not the spirit world.

At the end of August, the restaurant's bartender had a fight with the boss and quit. Since I often assisted her and knew how to mix drinks, I was promoted to the official bartender position. At first, it was fun. Behind the bar, I had a different identity. Men came in during quiet afternoons to pour their hearts out. I heard stories of romance, reconciliations and depression. They really needed a therapist, but the person behind the bar listened to all their problems for only a small tip.

Although I was open to finding a new life, I didn't know what I was looking for, and my wandering, gypsy lifestyle was filled with the wrong people. Monotony set in. No one ever went to the island's largely empty museum or did anything except drink and party. Jaywalking laws were strictly enforced, so even with no cars in sight, I had to stand at the corner and wait, holding in check my Manhattan impulse to rush across the street. The only challenge was learning Pig Latin because some of the natives I knew used it as their secret language. I needed more of a challenge than learning Pig Latin.

Toward the end of the summer, I dated Andre, a sophisticated French customer who lived in Manhattan. An intelligent conversationalist, he was my oasis from the local superficiality. We flew in a small plane to the island of Maui and spent the weekend at a scenic Sheraton Hotel. Although I enjoyed his company, we knew it wouldn't last. He had been made a eunuch from a painful castration while fighting in the Algerian War.

The bartending job was never planned as a lifetime career. I wasn't meeting people with shared interests. Earlier friends were missed and I yearned for the cultural opportunities of Manhattan. Then a letter arrived announcing that my New York roommate, Linda, was marrying her boss in October. It pointed me back to Manhattan and I was ready to return. I didn't derived energy from Hawaii, and the signposts were pointing back home. I boarded the plane to San Francisco, wanting to first see the town I had heard so much about. Then I would visit a friend in Sacramento.

A friendly gal about my age sat next to be on the bus when heading to San Francisco from the airport. We had a fun chat. She kindly invited me to stay with her friends and see the sights. Her friends took us everywhere, from Chinatown to the topless bars. It was easy to see why the picturesque city with rolling hills and exciting entertainment captured people's interest. I definitely wanted to return there at a later date.

If friends invited me to visit, I often showed up, pitched in with any work, and tried to make it a fun time for everyone. Carol, a girl I met on a chair lift in Aspen, had graciously invited me to visit her home in Sacramento. We first toured her city and then drove to Lake Tahoe for a weekend with a group of her companions. Eight convivial friends cooked a delicious meal that evening while we talked and laughed for hours. Having heard about Lake Tahoe as a famous ski resort, I pictured the lush mountain greenery covered in white snow.

Back in Sacramento, the newly-released Neil Simon movie *Barefoot in the Park* was playing. It was hilariously funny and the perfect ending to my trip. The Manhattan movie setting brought pangs of nostalgia flooding over me. Events conspire, and the next adventure follows. The cards came up for my life-changing episode in Manhattan.

Traveling for a year was terrific. I felt renewed. Wanderlust was finally out of my system. As I reflected upon my numerous adventures, something was missing. The explorations were all in my head, without a companion to bring them alive again. I wanted to find a good man to share my future voyages—a seemingly simple goal.

Chapter 11

My Lucky Break

Manhattan appeared more magical than ever, and I knew it was where I belonged. Endless opportunities for diversion and riches abounded. Excitement and energy pulsed through the streets in the fall of 1967. Flower children and marijuana now appeared everywhere. Birth control created a new freedom cry. Gloria Steinem's women's movement burned bras to protest inequality, and women wanted freedom from a restricting society. For the first time, the horrors of war with returning body bags were displayed in full color on living room televisions. Anti-war groups protested the draft that forced unwilling men to fight in Viet Nam—a war with questionable motives.

Although many people were sympathetic to some protestors, they did not join them for various reasons. Some worked better quietly behind the scenes. Many other priorities screamed for my attention.

I first needed to get settled and find a job. I began by freelancing as a temporary graphic artist in art studios. All freelance work was found through word-of-mouth referrals and treated by employers as an independent contractor. After several months, one of my freelance places offered a staff position, and I accepted.

Linda and her friends referred Sandra to me as a new roommate and we found a two-year, one-bedroom sublet in a modern building on East 70th Street. Sandra had recently left a teaching job on Long Island to become a buyer at Saks Fifth Avenue. Ricki, her distant acquaintance from teaching, was added later.

Our neighborhood hangout was The Beach, a friendly restaurant on the corner of 70th and Second Avenue. Bill and Tom, the owners, befriended the customers—creating a congenial atmosphere. Women as well as men felt comfortable dropping by after work.

By now, the drug culture was everywhere, and I was curious—as were others. I had my first real experience with what I think was concentrated marijuana pills on an unplanned visit by some friends to our apartment. The first pill had no effect, so I took another. Then a hanging birdcage began moving around, creating delightful designs in the air. This was followed by a potted plant turning into a small forest with people walking through it. The strange, surreal experience only lasted ten minutes. I saw how easily people could get hooked on the dopamine high, but I liked being in control of myself and did not want to start an addiction. All future offers were rejected, and the craving for duplication faded. If I was at a party, I would go back to the old cigarette trick and just take it to my lips without inhaling.

My new roommate, Sandra, was strikingly glamorous, always appearing as though she had just walked off the pages of a Saks Fifth Avenue catalog.

When she came into a room, men's heads would turn. Friends asked if she made me insanely jealous every morning. Although far from her glamour, I had my personal successes by then, so I answered, "I'm not the jealous type." I watched and learned from her, even if I didn't look like her. An early Martha Stewart, everything Sandra touched or cooked belonged in a magazine. She groomed herself to find a wealthy man. It was a foregone conclusion that she would have the perfect-life with the fairy tale ending.

Unfortunately, we didn't travel in the right social circles for her lavish tastes, so she met and married Bill, a handsome guy who had promise. His father and grandfather owned a small insurance company, which seemed substantial. I was a bridesmaid in a charming, picture perfect wedding. The fairy tale seemed to be happening. None of us anticipated the twists of fate to follow. After several years of marriage, they divorced.

While Sandra was engaged and married, I spent summer weekends visiting the Hamptons on Long Island. I first joined a low-budget group house of fun people. They piled eighteen people into a three-bedroom beach house on Dune Road in Westhampton. Mattresses were separated from their box springs to form beds for the women, while the guys utilized the couches or put sleeping bags on the floor. Everyone pitched in on the work for brunch on the porch and delicious, barbecued dinners.

Although most didn't know each other before the summer, it turned out to be a compatible group of young professionals. Everyone had to be easygoing to even join a house like that. Since it was mainly outdoor beach living, conditions were manageable and provoked many laughs.

It was there that I met Diana, a blond woman around my height. She was a talented designer at ABC Networks and I was working in a graphic design studio. We had a lot in common and became close friends.

Back in the city, Giora, a good-looking, dark-haired man of German-Italian heritage, came into my life. While I enjoyed his company, he didn't feel like my mate. There wasn't that special spark. Unfortunately, romantic chemistry is not controlled by logic. I was honest about my feelings, and we remained friends for a number of years. I am very grateful for our fun times together and his friendship. He played a pivotal role in my career and destiny. Before Giora, I had no plans to start my own business.

As International Advertising Manager for a major corporation, Giora controlled all the graphic design and advertising. He suggested that I approach my employer about getting a commission to bring some of his business into the design studio. My employer, the design studio owner, readily agreed, but I naively didn't ask for anything in writing. I thought my tightfisted boss would be fair and give me the going rate. I must have appeared as a guileless, pliant girl who could be pushed around. He gladly took the business but stalled and stalled—never paying a commission. It took me a lot of hits to prepare for the worst while hoping for the best in people.

Giora disclosed, "Your boss is telling me to bypass you with the assignments, and you are being excluded from the account." At Giora's urging, I quit and took the account with me. Giora was my lucky break. His guidance was the spark, and my frustration was the push to put my business in motion. I didn't hesitate to quit my job and embark on the next motivating adventure.

I was capable of all the work being assigned to my employer, and Giora knew it. I just hadn't thought about doing it independently. My assignments were peripheral studio work, and the advertising agency was still used for major projects.

The account brought waves of work. At times, I was overloaded and needed to hire extra help. Other times, business was quiet, so I was free to find other clients and freelance around the city.

Swirling thoughts mixed with my lucky break of having a good account. Inspiration struck! I knew I could create a professional central locating agency to connect business with freelance talent. It would solve my need to hire others for my projects as well as create commissions from other people's labor.

In my early Gal Friday job at Grey Advertising, I made frantic phone calls to find freelancers for rush jobs because there was no agency to call. I realized this could be my life-changing opportunity. An agency would serve both freelancers and clients. Many creative people don't like to sell themselves and are not adept at business.

I was thrilled when it all came to me. After work, I met up with my Aspen buddy Joan to tell her my plans. We met at the *Tin Lizzy,* a popular restaurant and bar near the *Time-Life* building. Whitey Ford, the famed Yankee pitcher, and Rocky Graziano, the World Middleweight prizefighter, happened to be sitting near us at the bar that night. Overhearing my enthusiastic new business announcement and excited description, they came over to introduce themselves. My startup idea hit a home run when they toasted to my business success!

Of course, getting the idea is just the first step. I had no concept of the complex road ahead.

The early business started with a small classified ad placed in the *New York Times* saying, "Wanted: A small good staff that likes to work independently." The phone rang incessantly. I set up appointments to review portfolios every half hour. Appointments waited in the reception area of my apartment building and were announced by the doorman through an intercom. When ready, I told the doorman to send them up, gave the applicant a simple application requesting references and answers to a few questions, and the request to sign a simple three-sentence contract. After reviewing their portfolio, I made notes and graded the candidate's skills for future use.

When companies called me for assignments, I introduced the new agency and asked if I could send someone else to do the job. As long as the job was done correctly, everyone was happy. I did the billing and collected a commission. I had no business plan, no capital, and no training. Since this was an innovative business model, there were no precedents to follow. The first contract was a simple three sentences, but awareness of other numerous issues made it grow to a complex ten-point agreement drawn up by a lawyer.

Diana, the designer from my first group house, and I planned to be partners when I could get the business to a point where she could quit her job. She suggested that her employer, ABC Networks, hire some of my freelancers, and I was able to provide her with some freelance design projects.

Diana and I were both artists with the ambitious dream of making millions, but neither of us knew anything about running a business or had investment capital. I made enough to support myself by handling what came in over the transom, but not to advertise and expand.

Contemporaries thought the business was a great idea, although potential dating partners sometimes found it threatening. I often underplayed what I did instead of selling the idea. It still loomed in the back of my mind that Prince Charming would change my life someday.

I was confused instead of certain about my future, so lacked any urgency to make money. Luckily "Creative Freelancers" was the only agency of its kind in town. It thrived as a small business by word-of-mouth.

Chapter 12

Twenty-something in Manhattan

Ms. Magazine first appeared as an inset in New York Magazine in December 1971 and became a separate magazine in 1972. I incorporated my company in 1970. Although I heard about the new feminist magazine and considered contacting the editors, I foolishly didn't. The magazine, co-founded by Gloria Steinem, famous journalist and activist, spotlighted women on the cover in 1976, and I should have been one of them. I always preferred fortune to fame, perhaps resulting from childhood training not to steal the spotlight from men. I needed a mentor who would make me realize fame was the fast track of fortune. Instead, my busy company always had emergency job orders to fill and social events beckoned. It was easy to put off making a contact that would have changed my life.

New York is a city that shifts on a dime from the elegant to the seedy. The landscape includes Broadway theaters, global business headquarters, outstanding museums, and charming ethnic neighborhoods. Friends and dates often headed to Chinatown or Little Italy for delicious dinners at affordable prices. Delicious food filled Little Italy's street festivals. Greenwich Village offered a night out with counterculture hippies and "beatniks" left from the Beat Generation literary movement of the 1950s. Summer festivals, such as the city's free professional productions known as *Shakespeare in the Park*, attracted thousands of peaceful onlookers.

In this era, when many young professionals, including myself, wanted to have fun as singles. We postponed getting married until as late as possible.

Soon after my return to the city, Larry entered my life. He was a skier with a friend who owned a two-engine, four-person plane. We had active weekends and some thrilling times. The pilot, Jack, and his girlfriend provided private plane transportation to their chalet and our skiing at Stowe, Vermont. One night we flew around Manhattan, below the height of the Empire State Building. The glittering city lights beneath us were unforgettably breathtaking. We glided carefully between buildings—above a vast expanse of city lights, before returning to the airport.

I found knowing the pilot and watching the small radar screen comforting, especially when we took off in snowstorms or hit bumpy spots of bad weather. One night we were flying back to Teterboro Airport with a blizzard below us. As we approached, the airport radio control tower warned of a dangerously low cloud ceiling with only 300 feet of visible area below the clouds. We nervously descended into the murky darkness. There was zero visibility at the windows. Suddenly, the pilot looked very anxious and rapidly tried all the controls. There was something wrong, and we didn't dare ask.

101

After an eternity of silence, Jack, said "This is it!" We braced for a crash. As the clouds ended, the lights quickly appeared on an icy runway. We bumped and skidded, eventually going off the runway and down a hill. A cheer went up when the plane gradually slowed to a stop. "We're alive!" It was only then we learned the damage. The control radio and one of the two engines was lost from slush and ice. Remarkably, we landed safely with just one engine and plane instruments.

Thankfully, Jack was an experienced pilot who never drank for twenty-four hours before flying. Larry, not one to be shy about asking questions, asked Jack how he had the money for a plane. Jack replied he was a distant relative of Howard Hughes. Years later, I saw a photo of Howard Hughes. Jack had the same eyes and they looked alike.

I knew from the beginning that Larry wasn't my marriage partner. He was attractive but pushy, and there wasn't a natural understanding between us. However, I was in my prime and exasperated that Prince Charming hadn't appeared so vulnerable. Larry asked me out for dinner. He was an enjoyable conversationalist who encouraged my new company and business discussions. His father had run a business, so was knowledgeable about many issues. I gave up on finding my dream soul mate and finally lost my virginity at the age of twenty-five. While I would have preferred to be in love, that didn't seem to be in my destiny. Larry was just at the right place at the right time.

He was also at the right place when I was moving apartments. Having my office at home created eligibility for a professional rent-controlled apartment.

I found a spacious residence in an architecturally noteworthy ten-story building on West 78th Street for only $309 a month. Even in those days, it was a deal. The apartment had bay windows, two large bedrooms, a full dining room, a pantry, plus two and a half baths and a cedar closet. There was no doorman, but the building had double-locked doors and was on an attractive city block behind the Museum of Natural History.

I had no furnishings. Larry supplied a dining room set that he couldn't use. He suggested moving his other furniture into my apartment and we live together temporarily while he was selling his house in a divorce. I foolishly agreed. Larry had a comfortable situation, so made various excuses not to move out. I couldn't throw him out so took a vacation by myself to the Club Med in Martinique. Told him if he wasn't gone by the time I got back, I would call the police.

His emergency phone call summoned me during night to the central office. I had to walk a sizeable distance in the jungle to the landline phone, as there were no cell phones back then. His call was a threat to commit suicide. My French Club Med roommate quickly put me at ease by announcing in a dismissive French accent, "Don't worry. People that commit suicide rarely announce it."

He was still alive and not out of the apartment upon my return, so I moved in with Diana and told him, "The police will get you out." He finally got the message and left. It taught me never to live with a man, even temporarily, unless planning marriage. A merged home life can be just as difficult to break up as a marriage, but without any benefits.

From then forward, I used a roommate service for my second bedroom. Candidates with references could be interviewed and I set the apartment rules. Unless an established friend, random acquaintances with unknown habits can be risky.

Connie was first, a dramatic, voluptuous brunette who had recently arrived in Manhattan from California. As an art therapist at Manhattan State Hospital, she tried to reintroduce mentally ill patients back to the world through art and music. In later years, I would take courses on frontiers of the human brain. My early memories created questions about brain chemistry.

One of Connie's autistic woman patients never talked but frequently stared at the piano. Connie repeatedly encouraged her to press the keys. After a couple of weeks, the woman sat down at the piano and played like a professional, then retreated back into her silent world. Although she couldn't communicate with people, her musical ability was unlocked.

As a kind person with virtuous values, Connie's mission was to bring these troubled people out of their own walled-off-from-life spaces. Unfortunately, she nurtured the wrong people in her personal dating life. Choices of much older or married men sabotaged her chances at romance, so she moved back to California after a sad heartbreak.

Sharon, Connie's replacement, was an intelligent gal with long reddish-blond hair. She came from a Scandinavian family of scientists in Arizona, had a chemistry degree, and was beginning a new job as a medical copywriter at a major medical advertising agency. Her scientific mind couldn't rationalize Christianity, but Sharon felt a strong need for traditions and spirituality. Assessing the three major religions in America at that time, she methodically picked Judaism as the most logical selection. Although Jewish custom tried to discourage converts three times, she was persistent—officially converting in Texas before deciding on New York for her career and as a likely place to find a Jewish husband. We remained roommates for five years and became lifelong friends.

One memorable night, when coming home from the ballet with a married girlfriend, Sharon mistakenly let a teenage couple into our building behind her. She then had second thoughts about getting into the same elevator with the couple and suggested to her friend that they take the stairs. The teenagers followed them into the staircase, pulled a knife and demanded their money and jewelry. Keeping a cool head, she gave them her wallet but didn't hand over most of her money, which was in the zipper pocket of her purse. Then the other girl pleaded for them not to take her wedding ring, so the robbers let her keep it.

Although they felt violated, Sharon and her friend arrived in the apartment laughing that their robbery had ended with everyone thanking each other. In typical Sharon fashion, she wrote it up in a story titled "An Avoidable Mugging" and posted it in the elevator. Her writing style was poignant and entertaining. However, we had some radically liberal neighbors on the top floor that wrote back, "These people are poor, and we should gladly give them our money." Sharon disagreed and felt she had been the violated victim of the robbery.

We were both pragmatic, but Sharon had a writer's skillful way of putting thoughts into flowing words. She also had a lot of common sense and people skills. I will always remember her pragmatic philosophy about dealing with problems. She said, "Accept your problems as your life. If we really knew what other people went through, we would pick our own situation as our skills are best suited to cope with familiar predicaments."

Our lifestyles blended, and we respected each other's personal space. She hunted for Jewish dates in Manhattan on summer weekends while I enjoyed the Hamptons' scene. On many occasions, we had fun in Manhattan together.

Sharon knew her own mind and pursued goals relentlessly. Eventually successful in her quest, she met and married Alex, a caring Jewish man from New York. Shortly after the wedding, they moved to the Midwest, where Sharon would study to become a therapist. Eventually receiving a doctorate, she moved with her husband to California, becoming a mother of two and family psychologist—the perfect career for her personality.

During the oppressively hot summer days, people scurried in a mass exodus from Manhattan to various destinations. Rental houses, ranging from small cottages to large mansions, were divided into group shares for fun and affordability. My group houses had mostly upwardly mobile young businesspeople in finance, advertising, or major corporations. Everyone was college-educated, made a decent living and enjoyed the good life. We expected to stay young forever. While lounging by the ocean or chatting at parties, conversations revolved around various current activities, including tennis, beach volleyball, bridge, backgammon, boating, cricket and golf.

In the winter, athletic singles were often enticed to participate in Vermont ski houses. Companionship on the slopes was combined with fondue socializing by the fireside and delicious, hearty dinners. After skiing for a winter in Aspen, the Vermont weather and icy conditions took significant adjustment, but it was better than not skiing.

While my first Hampton group house experience was a crowded, small house in Westhampton Beach, I soon became intrigued by the majestic mansions inhabited by other young professionals. They rented grand estates and hosted Great-Gatsby-style lawn parties. Before joining, I was told that the women must be willing to cook meals for large groups. A summer weekend schedule was prepared with an assigned woman captain and a man to assist with the shopping and chopping. Everyone pitched in for peripheral chores. I was okay with the task, and while a pretty good cook by then, the food in these houses was spectacular. I learned a lot more about gourmet cooking for large crowds.

Janet, our house organizer and grand dame of the Westhampton singles scene, organized the first lavish black-tie lawn party. Other large group houses soon followed. These elegant events in regal-looking homes offered tempting appetizers served on silver trays, beautiful floral decorations and live bands.

The formal evening parties were magical. Women in long dresses and men in white jackets roamed the party looking for laughs and sparks of romance. Hundreds of guests meandered about on the lawns. Others swirled the dance floor in elegant dresses or danced freestyle when the tempo picked up. The possibility of an ideal romance existed, but rarely happened.

Women seemed to expect an enchanted evening when a special stranger would walk across the room, ask them to dance, and their life would be lived happily ever after. However, most of the men had it too good to settle for one woman and didn't want to get branded as taken. Men didn't have to worry about the approaching end of childbearing years. Marriage meant estrangement from this fun singles scene, and many just wanted to have fun without commitment.

Most dating was in the city and not visible at the beach house—although guys would occasionally bring dates with them from the city. One couple in our house dated secretly for three winters, but acted like passing friends in the Hamptons during the summers. They finally married and are still together today. Some success stories happened, but it seems a small percentage, and many from the group never married.

I wanted to find a long-term companion who could share my life, although raising children appeared as an unwanted inconvenience until my late twenties.

A couple of notable men appeared on the horizon. One gross but funny situation happened with John, an attractive public defense lawyer with a big heart and small wallet. Defending those in society who couldn't afford help was very admirable, but I still wanted to live in Manhattan with a family. My everyday creature comfort needs were greater than his, but I was willing to compromise, feeling my business could grow to cover many of the costs.

Then those awful bugs appeared! One weekend we went to visit his sister and her friend in the mountains. They were building a house and we would lend a hand. It was a surprise to find the house full of dead flies. It had become infested with flies during the winter, and although exterminated in the spring, piles of dead flies were left everywhere. I dutifully swept the bugs into huge mounds and cleaned but was totally repulsed by the situation. He wanted to stay in the house for the night in sleeping bags, but I was unwilling. The place would give me nightmares. I insisted on sleeping in my car by myself, so we drove home. I had dreams about the dead flies for weeks to come. That was our last date. We both realized that it wouldn't work.

Abusive relationships can be difficult to detect at first. I should have seen Tom immediately as toxic and gone the other way. A small temper appeared that got worse with time. I appeased him for a while and tried to leave gracefully, but he always found excuses to drag the relationship out longer. One time he tested how I would react in a friendly wrestling match, and quickly realized not to mess with me; he might get kicked where it hurt, and the relationship would end. He never tried. I later found out that he had abused several women. He knew better than to physically abuse me. Never let them think you are weak.

Turning thirty is an auspicious time for women because it proclaims the better childbearing years are declining. I turned thirty at the same time as five other women friends. We celebrated with a group party for all in the Hampton house. Soon after, an old lady chased me in a dream, and I kept pushing her to the ground. I feared becoming that old lady, alone and without a family. I could no longer procrastinate the time for children. A decision that many women realized much earlier was finally reached. I would follow my mission statement by seriously considering the interested men and then playing the best card I could.

Rob came into my life at a Thanksgiving dinner in South Hampton while I was dating Tom. Rob was an attractive man who had everyone roaring with laughter from his entertaining stories. Tom and I ran into him again at a supermarket out in Westhampton on a subsequent weekend. Rob was with Helga, an attractive Swedish gal displaying her 42 D cleavage by buttoning her blouse around her navel. Neither of the men liked each other, so Tom was quick to point out that Helga was the type of woman Rob usually dated.

Nonetheless, I convinced Tom to invite them both to our dinner party that weekend and he acquiesced. The meal was a casual evening of lasagna and salad for fourteen people. I liked lasagna because it could be made in advance, letting me enjoy the party. Rob attended but complained to others how lasagna was a cheap meal. People commented that he was rudely insensitive, but I was foolishly forgiving. However, I ended the Tom relationship.

Rob and I saw each other the following summer at a gathering in the Hamptons. Using the lure that he might use some of my freelancers, Rob invited me to his office. He owned a design and production firm that produced displays and exhibits. After I gave my pitch at his impressive midtown Manhattan office, we went out for lunch.

Chapter 13

The Cards That Were Dealt

Rob was an attractive, articulate designer with a great sense of humor who told animated stories about his business travels around the world. He partnered with his brother in a design business specializing in dimensional design for exhibits and point-of-purchase displays. The company fabricated several world's fair pavilions and employed eleven people in New York City. Rob seemed financially secure. Moreover, he wasn't threatened by my business, and complimented my sales weakness. I presumed his business would continue to take him all over the world and could provide a good family income.

Here was a financially-stable man who had raised three children in Manhattan and had no desire for the suburbs. Two of his three daughters were in private New York high schools and one at the University of Tampa. His marriage failure was blamed on an alcoholic wife who was having an affair.

In retrospect, part of my attraction to Rob was his Irish gift for words and freedom from inhibitions. His impressive knowledge of politics and history—along with amusing storytelling—captured people's attention. Selling was a natural extension of his personality. My more reserved heritage made me talk myself out of action by "analysis, analysis, and paralysis."

I assumed he was in his late thirties or forty at the most, as he was very energetic and had a youthful appearance. After a couple of dates, I found out he was 49, seventeen years my senior. I candidly told him, "I'm looking to have children, and you are too old."

Nothing intrigues a man's interest more than a wanted catch that tries to get away. His ego couldn't handle the fact that I might pick someone else, so he persistently used all his sales ability to persuade me otherwise. I continued to date him because he was a lot of fun, but I had met someone else with potential, so I was on the fence. Rob told a convincing story about how he enjoyed children and really missed not spending more time with his first family. People hear what they want to hear, and I was no different. I lost interest in the other guy and started to believe that age didn't make much difference.

We set a year as the deciding time, and if all went well, marriage would follow. The following year was filled with dinner parties, friends and all the excitement Manhattan had to offer. In August, we made serious plans to be married the following January, and I looked forward to our life together.

Rob's Manhattan apartment on Sutton Place was elegantly decorated with fabric wallpaper and treasured antiques. His beach house on Dune Road in Westhampton was more eclectic but suited the environment. The house had an idyllic setting with a boat and dock in the backyard bay and a beach with white sands touching rolling ocean waves a short walk across Dune Road. It had been purchased back in the 1950s as a small place to go for water-skiing, but over the years Rob expanded the house to five bedrooms.

This blue wood house was nestled amid trees, dusty miller plants and dune grass. Red geraniums dotted the window box and doors. Wild daisies were often in a living room vase. It was a simple house with finished wood floors, but the dining room had an unusual gambrel-shaped roof, deep paisley wallpaper, and a large extendable blue table. Two huge sconces and a large, artistically abstracted nude hung on the walls. The ambiance was especially delightful by candlelight.

Its vibrant setting was enhanced by a dock for his water-skiing boat and frequent skiers. In the summers, a couple of rooms were rented out to friends to provide companionship and cover expenses. He required that the men be willing to water-ski and the women help with the cooking. High tide always brought other friends, eager to go out for a ski and socialize, some staying for dinner. Wine flowed with laughs as we watched sunsets over the bay and smelled sizzling steaks on the charcoal grill.

His family was friendly, always full of jokes and laughs. Ann, Rob's younger sister, was ten years older than me and married to a wealthy entrepreneur. Ann staged huge parties and charity events in Bloomfield Hills, Michigan, where she lived with her husband and children.

Clint, his younger brother, was the inside administrative man for the business, while Rob did the concept design and sales. Their father had started the business many years before as a printing company— putting his sons in equal partnership. Rob loved design and turned the company into an award-winning design firm.

Money didn't seem to be a problem. Some years before I came on the scene, their parents had sold a large home in the Hampton area. Others told me that Rob would have a large inheritance when his parents died because their Hampton house was valuable and his father had been a successful businessman. His parents rented an attractive Manhattan Eastside apartment and took us out for dinner at impressive restaurants on Thanksgiving and special occasions.

The key ingredients for a marriage partner were there. Young and ready for challenges, I felt my skills and problem-solving ability could withstand whatever destiny had put into my path. Moreover, while often self-absorbed and not a good listener, Rob was a good dancer. Even though he could be bombastic and oblivious to my feelings, it seemed a gamble worth taking for the family and companionship I craved.

Marriage was at a critical fork in the road, and neither the single or married path promised the perfect life. I decided to take my chances with marriage.

Set the mind, and the heart will follow. I had a heart full of love, so in my mind, Rob became the right person to receive it. I rationalized that many women didn't meet their soul mates and married suitable mates instead, with some even having mates picked by parents. I was determined that my marriage would succeed.

During our year and a half of dating, I ignored warning signs. I either joked about Rob's insensitivities or corrected them. He would usually adapt if a blunder was pointed out. One of his friends tried to warn me, "Rob is not right for you. Why are you with him?" I didn't listen. I thought most difficulties could be overcome by my determination. I had grown up with a father and brother who weren't interested in my feelings, so I didn't realize the importance of easy two-way communication and empathy as a requirement for marriage relationships.

The beginning of the marriage voyage came with a mixture of sunshine and stress. Unexpected storms showed up. A few months prior to the wedding, my mother's arm went numb, and she had a dreadful stroke, leaving her crippled. An incompetent doctor worsened her condition, and soon after Christmas, my worst nightmare happened. Mom had her fatal stroke. Had she regained consciousness, she would have been in a vegetable state. Instead, she died early in January at age 71. It was devastating, and my tears seemed unstoppable, but I had to go forward with my life and business.

Despite working in Vaudeville chorus lines, Mom had remained a quintessential, small-town girl who never lost her engaging charm. She was the most gracious, kind and humble person I've ever known, and I still miss her dearly. Being more suited to the dream of motherhood than show business, Mom had as much a career as wanted before her marriage at age thirty. She gladly embraced being a wife and mother. Steady and firm, only demanding what was generally fair, she often exclaimed punishing children hurt her more than the child. Knowing her has aided my ability to recognize good people and to believe in altruism.

I considered canceling the wedding planned for January 17th when Mom had a second, final stroke. With my father's consent and a heavy heart, I went ahead with the plans. Due to my mother's illness and

Rob's complex family situation, it had been prearranged as a small, private church wedding. Only eight friends would attend the ceremony with brunch afterward at the Plaza Hotel. In attendance on the cold but sunny day in January were my ski buddy, Joan; her husband, Bob; our beach house companions, Pam and Richard; and Rob's longtime friends, Jill, Bob, Inez, and Fred.

We invited some family and close friends to an evening party at our apartment, without telling them we were getting married. Our guests were astounded by the news as they entered the door. There had been no mention of an engagement or even the possibility of marriage. No one other than my father and the wedding party was informed.

During the evening, my new mother-in-law asked, "When do you plan to stop working? It is the man's job to support his family." Her idea of a woman's financial survival was leaving it to the man. She came from poor Irish immigrant roots and had struggled as a model until rescued by her husband, who gave her a comfortable life.

I had no desire or intention to stop work. My mother-in-law never had anything to lose, but I did. My business was a living entity with employees. I had brought it into the world and nurtured it daily. It had grown to be part of my identity. A lot of hard work goes into building a company's reputation, and I wouldn't just walk away. My generation cheered me on, but she found my choice hard to understand.

Moreover, living in Manhattan is high-priced, and throwing your financial security onto someone else can be a gamble. I could foresee my income becoming needed. She was also shocked that I would keep my maiden name for my business because it had industry recognition.

Neither Rob nor I could take time off from our businesses in January for a week-long honeymoon vacation. A previous partially business trip to France and the island of Corsica on Thanksgiving weekend was considered our pre-honeymoon. The day after the wedding was spent at a Super Bowl party, and then we returned to work.

I officially moved into his apartment—giving up my West Side rental, which was larger and had lower rent. However, Sutton Place was much more elegant and prestigious.

Pam and Richard, who were at our wedding ceremony and good friends from summers at the beach house, gave us a fabulous party in their newly-purchased, large co-op apartment on Fifth Avenue. While at our beach house, Pam had begun a new business that had become hugely successful. Despite learning difficulties that had hampered her in school, she had an eye for color and design that paid off as an entrepreneur.

When Pam had reached a glass ceiling at her publishing job, she cleverly put her personal design taste into a wicker furniture store on upper Madison Avenue. Her favorite colors were Kelly green, pink, yellow and white. The store floor was painted a shiny, bright Kelly green. White wicker furniture was placed on the stunning green floor and decorated with cushions covered in tasteful, pink, yellow and green printed patterns. It made a striking impression. The press came for an opening party, and she became an immediate hit. Later, she purchased the building and added a clothing store for children—based on the same colors.

Pam's determination to succeed was spurred by her high school teachers saying that she wasn't college material. She resolved to prove their comments wrong by successfully completing her degree and working hard. Pam's success story inspired me in later years when raising children with difficulties.

My wedding was a turning point in many ways. I was shocked and saddened that two very close friends had dropped out of my life when they got the news. Diana, my best friend and business associate, never showed at the party or even sent a card. Rob explained that she had made a calculated pass at him a few months before. She must have felt guilty about stabbing me in the back. Trust was destroyed but if she had just come clean and apologized, I would have forgiven her for the first offense. A few years earlier, I had given Diana a wedding shower and flown to Florida for her ceremony. She had married after a three-month courtship and divorced a year later.

Giora's reasons were more understandable. He was obviously very disheartened that I had married. It was difficult to see them both go.

The second storm came on the horizon less than a month after our wedding. Rob's ex-wife was diagnosed with lung cancer. She wouldn't accept that her cancer might be fatal and refused to sign the legal papers brought to her hospital bed by her friend and lawyer. Many new decisions had to be made about the future of Rob's children and finances.

By summer, I desperately needed some time to unwind. My mother's death, the loss of friends, and new family responsibilities were a lot to hold inside.

As the weekend group left for the city on Sunday night, I assured everyone that I just needed some quiet time. Four days were spent alone at our beach house, trying to make sense of it all and reprogramming my dreams for the future. It wasn't the newlywed year I had envisioned.

First, I needed time to grieve for my mother and regain strength. My pain from her loss was deeply buried, and the floodgates had to open. I had tried to save her but ran into a wall of old-fashioned attitudes about doctors. My parents would only trust their local doctor, who didn't prescribe the correct medication. Moreover, cortisone pills given for her arthritis had disastrous effects. She rarely took medications, and the moon-faced drug reactions occurred, puffing up her face. When I came for a visit, she was in pain and crying—sitting in a dark room with her face swollen double the average size. She could barely see.

It broke my heart to observe her this way, but I was powerless to change anything. She said, "I always thought that if I were a good person, life would be fair to me in the end." What was happening wasn't what she envisioned or deserved. Her words have always haunted me. I lost a part of myself. Death has the capacity to penetrate every last cell of those who remain.

Dad was distraught with her loss and finally changed doctors. He commented, "The doctor never even visited the hospital." I wasn't surprised.

I thought ahead to my new life and challenges. Becoming a stepmother, plus raising my own children in Manhattan, would be a monumental task. I was about to get a lot more responsibility than anticipated and would have to rise to the occasion. My Prince Charming would need a lot of help.

I walked over the dune grass covered hills of sand on an old wooden walkway to a beach, which opened up to display miles of sand on either side with an ocean horizon that dropped off into eternity. Seagulls sounded my arrival, perhaps hoping for food, and then joined their group in an established pecking order. As I collected seashells and contemplated the view, I thought of my early memories and wondered about eternity. The thundering of giant waves in front of stunning sunrises and sunsets still remain fixed in my mind. While the time there was short, it was enough to give some perspective for what lay ahead.

Chapter 14

Friendly Chaos

Rob's ex-wife's only words to me were, "Take care of my girls." We met once at the Hamptons the summer before she was diagnosed. I later wondered if she may have known something was wrong with her health. Rob's marriage had ended ten years before I arrived into his life.

Her life ended that October at age forty-nine when she died of lung cancer. She was a smoker and alcoholic. Although she received sufficient income from child support and alimony payments, plus had liquid assets left from their family home, she canceled her medical insurance and refused to sign a will. Without a legal will or health insurance, most of her remaining money went to pay medical and probate costs.

Each daughter inherited about the equivalent of a nice car or two years at college, plus some gold jewelry and their home's furnishing. The girls were still very immature, but there were no restrictions on usage. Their mother's lawyer was watching, and Rob couldn't do anything except let them have it.

121

Rob's first plan was to leave his daughters living in the same apartment on 79th Street, where they lived with their mother and childhood nanny, who had a free room and another job. This would have been the equivalent of letting teenage girls live on their own in Manhattan, as their sweet nanny was no match for these three active, vivacious, and pretty teens. While Rob didn't want his life disrupted, I knew they needed their father and stable home, so I said that plan was wrong. Since they were all away at school for most of the time, he agreed to have them move into our second bedroom. I didn't fully realize the complexity and daunting nature of the task ahead.

Rob was on a sailing trip in the Caribbean, leaving me with the chaos of three girls moving into our apartment that November. He couldn't cope and wanted to be far away. I was annoyed that he had left and disappointed with his attitude, but I tried to remain positive and be ready for my new role of stepmother.

My new adventure kicked off with their baggage filling the hallway in our apartment building on moving day. What couldn't be squeezed into our two-bedroom apartment was shipped to Long Island City for storage. It was mayhem, which I organized as well as possible.

I finally began to comprehend the formidable undertaking ahead. This was new terrain. My new stepdaughters were disorganized, untamed teenagers with lots of bad habits. Living would be chaotic in very tight quarters during holidays and school vacations when they were home. Luckily, the girls had a sense of humor and could make me laugh.

Laura, Jennifer and Allie loved to laugh and joke around. They had entertaining personalities but were strong-willed with powerful opinions, frequently arguing among themselves. Laura, a reddish-blond and the oldest, had a very high-energy personality. Jennifer, a beautiful natural light blonde, was the middle, more controlling sibling. Allie, the youngest, was a light brunette with a deep, warm, charismatic voice. She did not stand a chance in arguments against her sisters, so was easygoing.

I had married into a family with a very different lifestyle from my upbringing. The girls had been groomed as party girls who would hopefully marry rich men. Both Rob and his ex-wife preferred parties to domestic priorities, so they had ignored what they didn't want to see. Despite Rob's tactless comments and absences, his daughters loved him and clamored for their father's attention in any way possible.

Rob's Irish blarney trait walked a fine line between lies and storytelling. "Bullshitting" was his euphemistic word for lying to achieve an effect. His children learned early that they could evade the truth or make a joke out of their actions, so accountability seemed to be a lost concept.

From the girls' perspective, I was better than the other women he had dated for the previous ten years. They teased that I was an improvement over the long-term girlfriend with the hot temper who threw things across the room and the girlfriend with the blouse open much too low.

We had some laughs, and they joked about me being their stepmother by singing the mouse song from Cinderella. I tried my best to help where I could and provide a home environment. They were used to just grabbing food from the refrigerator, so they laughed about living like the "Brady Bunch" from the famous

TV sitcom when we sat down to dinner. However, most of their formative years were over. My presence was just a curiosity and learning experience for them.

When Allie's mother became terminally ill, it seemed a young teenager would be better off in an upbeat, supervised school environment than watching her mother's health deteriorate daily. We sent her to a charming New England boarding school for young girls during her last two years of high school.

Raising someone else's children was a significant task, and I was more comparable to an older sister. One evening when I was still new on the job, Allie wanted to go out at 10 p.m. to meet a girlfriend in Manhattan. In my judgment, this was too late for a 16-year-old to be heading out in Manhattan, but she and her father out-voted me, agreeing she would be back by midnight. Since it was the custom in my family to leave a light on until the person arrived home safely and was able to turn it out, I did so. Shortly after midnight, the light was still on. I slept lightly, waiting. It never went out. At 3 am, I was wide awake, worriedly pacing in the living room while her father slept soundly.

Finally, at 4 a.m., I called the other parents. They sleepily answered the phone. While a somewhat embarrassed by the situation, they concluded the girls were probably okay and would be home soon. At 5 a.m., Allie arrived home. Surprised to see me up, she was actually pleased to see someone cared.

Trying to change habits at that point, however, was practically impossible. I did my best in various situations, often failing. I think some helpful values and thoughts were instilled. I also provided a buffer for their father's insensitive comments and reactions by frequently intervening before their feelings were hurt.

I felt the closest to Allie of the three, as we had the most bonding time and conversations. I was running a business and knew I would never replace her mother, but I took the new responsibility seriously.

On our first Christmas together, three months after her mother died, Jennifer gave her father a framed picture montage from her mother and father's wedding for his gift. Her sisters laughed loudly, Rob and I remained silent, and she burst into tears. Jennifer meant it with sincerity and couldn't understand why it was insensitive to me and an unwanted present by her father. Rob was known to be equally stubborn and undiplomatic, so they often clashed.

Jennifer had a boyfriend for a few years, but she wasn't in love. With her inheritance, she quit college at the end of the spring semester, purchased a car and drove across the country to live in Ashland, Oregon, leaving her boyfriend and everyone else behind. We didn't see her again for several years.

Rob's finances were becoming very unreliable. His business was having severe problems, and he was getting older. He insisted that if his daughters were serious about getting an education, the money should go toward their last two college years. If he didn't do that, the inheritance cash would have been blown frivolously, and more loans would be needed to pay for college.

Laura, the oldest sibling, had been attending the University of Tampa in Florida, taking the required courses, plus some frivolous electives like "The Occult" and "Underwater Basket Weaving." When her mother died, and the tuition became her inheritance, she transferred to Boston University and took her education more seriously. However, time and therapy were needed for her to cope with her mother's death and the real world she now faced.

After completing all but three credits in her art degree, Laura decided to come home. I taught her the basic production skills needed for most entry positions in the commercial art industry at my office. Until computers transformed the graphics industry, art schools at universities resisted requiring courses in practical, production-oriented entry-level skills. Upon returning to Boston, she began her career as a graphic designer.

Allie had a deep, warm, charismatic voice. She chose a drama major at Ithaca College and took acting lessons in New York City. I was amazed at how Allie could memorize and deliver lines from Shakespeare and other plays.

Allie moved home while she took acting classes and auditioned for roles. She was a good actress but it was competitive. I gave her a job as the receptionist in my office. She moved on to a receptionist position for an advertising agency and won an industry award for an ad headline, while at the front desk. However, breaking into advertising was as competitive as acting. After a romantic break-up, Allie followed her sister, Laura, to Boston and became a promotion copywriter with Blue Cross.

Life looks better from behind a smile, and humor does lighten the tension. The man I married was a fun date, and that didn't change after marriage. He just lived in his own bubble, doing what he felt like doing. Rob's style was to joke about everything possible, and he used humor to his advantage. It took a year before he admitted he could make scrambled eggs because he didn't want to cook breakfast.

Days and nights were never dull. We gave or attended dinner parties almost every weekend at our Westhampton beach house from May through early November. As members of the Westhampton Country Club, we enjoyed club events, played with tennis groups and enjoyed dancing, both ballroom and freestyle. There were friendly bridge game evenings in Manhattan, plus frequent dinners at a favorite Irish pub. Conversations covered a wide range of subject matter, as Rob was well-read and connected to interesting people. His boundless energy included playing tennis all year and water-skiing when weather permitted. A short catnap was all he needed to recharge.

During the first summer of our marriage, Rob placed a bucket of under-sized flounder in front of me, caught on a fishing trip with his friends. He then demonstrated how to chop off their heads and prepare filets before going off to have drinks with his buddies. I tried to do one while drinking a glass of wine and wearing dark glasses, but couldn't stomach the job. I quietly put the bucket into the car and took it to the local seafood store.

They gladly exchanged it for the flounder filets that I needed for dinner. Everyone raved about the meal made "with the fish they caught." The shrimp-stuffed flounder with onions and cream sauce was delicious, and the guys filled the dinner time with humorous stories. My full story came out later, and I had the best laugh of the evening.

Another memorable time, he learned a lesson about not making plans for me without my consent. Rob was out in the Hamptons, spending the final week of August with his friends. I arrived late on Thursday afternoon for a much-needed long weekend. I hadn't taken any vacation. To my surprise, as I walked in the door, eleven people were arriving for dinner at his invitation.

He expected me to cook for everyone and thought everything could just be thrown together while he grilled the steaks. Dinner invitations were owed to some of the people sitting in our living room, but I neither wanted to cook dinner for everyone nor felt this was how I wanted to prepare for it. I pulled a stunt learned from a friend's wife on our earlier pre-honeymoon trip to Corsica, an island off the coast of France.

On the trip to France, we took a side-trip to Rob's longtime friend, Charles Levier, an entertaining, somewhat-crazy, successful French artist who had been married six times. He was living on the island of Corsica with his wife of eleven years. Their home was a charming, large French farmhouse. Animals would wander about the grounds, sometimes poking their heads into the kitchen. Charles' wife had been a beautiful model in her day but was now showing her years.

Our hosts knew we were coming, so organized a dinner party. We preferred to just be with our friends, but they insisted. About an hour before the guests arrived, Charles' wife had a headache and didn't come out of the bedroom all evening. I felt it was fake and probably just stress, as she was not used to entertaining and had a history of psychological problems.

She left me in charge of the cooking and socializing for a group of people who spoke only French. I used a glass of wine to help me remember some high school French and then added a French accent to Italian vocabulary from my semester abroad. It came out better than expected, enabling fundamental communications. Charles said, "Mar-e-lyn! When did you learn to speak French?"

This previous headache scene came immediately to mind when I walked in on Rob's surprise dinner group in the Hamptons. I immediately begged off, saying, "So sorry, but I have a bad headache and need to rest." The jovial group managed with Rob as the organizer for dinner. I didn't come out of the bedroom for the entire evening. He brought me food and didn't make that blunder again!

Marriage to Rob was an action-packed game-changer leading to unimaginable events. Family and business were full of challenges to conquer and parties to attend.

Chapter 15

Business Learning Curves

The life of an entrepreneur is a constant adventure. There are unlimited doors to open, things to learn and mountains to climb. I stumbled on a huge business opportunity, but it took a while before events converged to make me want to take control of the reins aggressively. The groundwork was laid before meeting Rob, but money to raise children was my ultimate motivation to make it grow.

Until I began "Creative Freelancers," non-staff employment was referred to as "free-lance" help—two words and hyphenated. The origination of the word free-lance goes back to medieval history, where it meant "a hired sword." Phil, a copywriter friend, and I were tossing around ideas for the company name one day. He said that "Creative Free-lance" wasn't grammatically correct. It would sound better as "Creative Freelancers." And so, the word "freelancers" was coined. In later years, the word became common language, and my competitors used it frequently. "Creative Freelancers Inc." was incorporated in 1970, and the full name was trademarked—never thinking of the word "freelancer" as a potential asset by itself.

After about a year of working out of my apartment, I sublet two offices from a small advertising agency on 60th Street and Madison Avenue. At a home office, work never takes a break. Clients thought nothing of calling in the middle of dinner or ten o'clock at night—expecting freelancers to appear the next morning. I needed a better balance in my life and was happy to use the office answering machine. Phone calls were sometimes made in the evenings, but clients didn't casually leave their job order until late hours.

Many freelancers applied for work, and my specialty was to discern those capable of being dropped into the middle of a rush assignment and performing well. The ability to do most of the skills myself enabled evaluations, often with an uncanny instinct for assessing which freelancer was perfect for the job. There were no computers for testing skills. Aptitudes had to be ferreted out by discussion, reviewing samples and checking references.

As the time grew closer to my marriage, it became apparent that my business would have a financial role. Until then, I had just thought about supporting myself and my fun activities. Making a lot of money had been an exciting concept, but the urgency wasn't there. However, it was now evident finding a very wealthy Prince Charming wasn't in my cards and my potential mate had a lot of expenses. He was also supportive of my role as a business owner.

While Rob seemed to make a decent income and have assets, it was not enough for three daughters in college and a larger family-size apartment in Manhattan. Moreover, a recent business climate change left the future of his finances uncertain. I found myself with a unique enterprise that was full of potential, and now there was growing pressure to make money for family support. How could it be done?

A newspaper ad led to an enlightening two-week MBA summary course at a midtown hotel. I signed up immediately and was the only woman in this crash program for businessmen. Each half-day summarized one curriculum class in a Master's in Business Administration. It was eye-opening. The classes taught about business plans, hiring staff and making things happen. These were exciting clues to reach my pot of gold. For years my company had drifted without a direction or plan.

Surprisingly, the class on statistics was my favorite and still stands out in my mind. Math was never one of my better subjects, but the teacher began the session with a deck of cards. He taught about the law of averages by flipping cards—concluding that if we picked carefully and hired the right people, the chances for success were high. He added when possible, giving qualified managers the capital for improvements had good odds for a solid return. The path sounded clear and attainable.

Other sessions were equally enlightening. Human resources stressed hiring qualified people as a critical component of success. Hiring to existing weaknesses was advocated. Skills need to be balanced, so it was considered wise to hire someone with abilities to make the company grow, not a friendly clone. In a new startup, there is no room for wasted salaries. My thirsty mind soaked up whatever it could learn.

Targeted advertising and promotion were the proven ways to get sales results. Basic marketing concepts and branding the company images were pinpointed as essential. Easy to understand concepts and images must be presented to the consumer. I was aware of promotion design from my art background, but the importance of discerning the specific audiences and how to brand the company helped establish my first sales brochure.

"Who's got the monkey?" That phrase was the subject of a business management class. It is hard to hold onto a troublesome monkey, so the monkey symbolized a problem that you don't want. People will keep piling monkeys on a manager's desk. Good managers must delegate by determining the best staff person to solve the situation and passing the monkey to that employee. The visual became engraved in my mind.

Of course, these were very condensed courses, just touching on subjects like accounting, finance and economics. The teachers were realistic but humorous with their lessons. At the end of the course, we reviewed the steps to develop a complete business plan and raise capital.

If you want to be successful, devise a big picture plan. While a formal business plan to raise capital is a significant endeavor, thinking about the goals and obstacles is simple, common-sense planning. It is essential to identify target objectives and problems that need solving. Composing a plan helps prepare for the future and provides a reference outline. I usually read and revise my business and personal plans at least yearly.

"Write down a clear picture of the industry's market potential and opportunity," advised the teacher. "Consider how to reach your customers. Once the goals are determined, analyze the competition. What strategy will make it profitable? Consider startup costs. Plan the roadmap."

"Work smart, not just hard. Have backup plans." The presumption of my class was that if you follow the rules of business, success follows. Experience has since taught that it is wise to have a Plan A, Plan B and Plan C prepared. Plan A is the goal, Plan C is how to cope with serious problems, and Plan B is probably where you will wind up. Be equipped for both good and bad luck. World events will create unimagined pitfalls and opportunities. The economy will influence business outcomes, while technology constantly changes the landscape. Entrepreneurs must use every skill available to make their venture flourish.

I knew "Creative Freelancers" was an excellent idea, so I was full of confidence as I dove into uncharted water. I applied for a loan at the Small Business Administration with a formal, detailed business plan. I didn't take into account that women entrepreneurs in business were relatively unknown and not encouraged.

I looked young and unlikely, plus the freelance industry was thought to be people out of work, not a recognized professional group. The reviewing agents couldn't think out-of-the-box. Without similar company models for comparing projected profits, I was rejected.

I pressed forward, following what was learned in the course and playing all my cards. I printed the first sales brochure and hired Robin, my first assistant. The company's size doubled in a year. The MBA course was minimal, but it helped. Today there are many more opportunities for self-motivated entrepreneurs, including extra help to women and minorities to obtain venture capital.

We make some choices, and others are made for us. I knew the costs of raising a second family in Manhattan would be steep, but Rob's big downhill turn was completely unexpected. The U.S. Trade Act of 1974 opened the way for free trade agreements with other countries, rendering Rob's prices uncompetitive with Canada. It was a slow poison, which killed off clients for his company.

Actions have a reaction. In government, one place benefits, and the other loses. Many of Rob's clients were foreign governments who wanted to exhibit at shows or stores in the U.S.—particularly the French and Italian governments. His company designed, produced and installed their trade show exhibitions and point-of-purchase displays. Now he lost bids for projects. His contacts also began to retire. Continuing existing accounts and new sales with higher prices became difficult to negotiate. The pressure continued to mount for me to turn "Creative Freelancers" into a larger money-maker.

"Sales" is the engine for business growth, but it was my weakest skill. Watching Rob was a superb course in salesmanship. His aggressiveness and entertaining style steered conversations to subjects that all sides would find useful. I was awed by the way he could find a helpful contact lead in the middle of every party. Never shy, he got their business card and followed up the next day.

Rob left no stone unturned when seducing a client, —relentlessly pushing the sale until he closed the deal or it fell apart. He knew the questions to ask and told potential customers what they wanted to hear. In a bar, at a party or on the street, he talked to anyone who seemed interesting. Rob had a memorable phone voice, which—combined with his humor and unique selling style—became engraved in people's minds. Confident from his earlier success, rejection never bothered him. Rob was a master at networking before they taught it in schools.

Dorset, one of his close friends, used to say, "When Rob calls, it's an invitation to go out and play." Rob could always regale people with tales of world travel, escapades building the world's fair pavilions, historical anecdotes, episodes with the CIA after WWII, and his water skiing. The entertaining times were generally welcomed. He unquestionably tried. However, the tide had turned against him, and he struggled against the flow of policy change.

I admired him for his strengths, which were my weaknesses. To make sales calls, I needed to first repeat to myself, "If nothing is ventured, nothing will be gained." Better to act first, letting confidence follow. Rob had the sales courage that I lacked. While generally supportive of my business and often passing out my promo cards, he was consumed with his own problems.

I kept turning over all the cards and tried to make sales for my company. With time I became more desensitized to rejections, but it didn't make me a strong salesperson. I would never have his style and could only sell from my heart. Still subconsciously frozen about putting myself out there, I refused public speaking offers. Being on a forum panel with questions was okay, but I was uncomfortable giving a prepared speech at luncheons and making a larger splash. It was lost free publicity.

I remembered the lesson in my MBA course about hiring to weakness. When first rejected for funding by the Small Business Administration, I had hoped a partner could be developed from within the company by offering commission incentives. However, a larger ball was needed. Since I couldn't afford a high salary, the person would have a stake in the profits.

Fulltime placement agency salespeople dealt with many of the same contacts as our freelance firm and functioned on sizeable commissions, so they seemed likely candidates. A classified ad in the *New York Times* tested who might be available. Barbara responded.

She had a strong, positive industry reputation as a well-known "headhunter" for advertising agencies. Barbara's gossipy chatter presented a telephone-style that intrigued clients and candidates alike. They would chat amicably, often supplying potential candidates and human resource contacts. I felt very lucky.

Hoping for a partner, I offered a commission split of 50/50, higher than the usual 60/40, plus supplied the office with support services. Each of us brought certain advertising contacts and business advantages to the table. Never doubting we would be successful, no agreement was put into writing.

Chapter 16

Jumping Hurdles

The hardest part of a business is always the start-up stage. Barbara pulled an immediate draw against commissions, which took at least three months for payment from her client to my company. I added Joanna, a salary plus commission placement assistant, at Barbara's suggestion. Toward the end of the first year, my energy and resources building the full-time placement division began to pay off.

Anticipating future growth, I found a six-office suite at 150 East 58th Street in the Architects and Designers Building, a city block from the famous Bloomingdale's Department Store and the Lexington Avenue subway. It was also within easy walking distance to my apartment. Rob supplied some office furniture from his office storage and helped decorate the reception room.

Barbara dropped the bomb just before the office move. She calmly explained her need for all the profit from any placement commissions to cover her personal expenses, so she was setting up her own office in competition. Moreover, Barbara was hiring Joanna away. After a year of effort and investment, she left me stranded with higher rent and no salesperson. I was plunged into a canyon and had to find my way out. Foolishly, I hadn't prepared well for the terrain change. How could I be so trusting and not get the deal in writing on my terms?

Competition for money has the nickname of a "rat race" for a good reason, and some of the rats travel in disguise.

I had to pay Joanna more to keep her from leaving, and then I had to be understanding with the frequent calls and emergencies from her four children. Joanna was a capable administrator, but she didn't have Barbara's contacts or chatter style. Strangers always thought she was the boss because of her matronly figure and deep theatrical voice. It was hard enough for the Syrian guards at the Embassy down the hall to accept a woman running a business, but it was clearly disturbing when they discovered it was run by a young woman—and not Joanna. In fact, we were about the same age, but I always looked ten years her junior. The bank also doubted my credibility, and was shocked when it was discovered I was the check signer.

Selfish people will do anything to get what they want. After Barbara, new employees became required to sign non-compete agreements, and I never trusted again when it came to money. Employees had relationships with our clients and knew our candidate lists—both potentially transferrable business assets.

In the race to the pot of gold, the runner faces hurdles. Focus enhances the chances of winning. An entrepreneur faces staff changes, competition, psychotics and new government regulations, among other factors. There can be a lot of fun adventures, but there are also dangerous, drooling hyenas and hungry killer sharks anywhere there is money. If you bravely enter the money arena, be careful.

When living in a jungle, also watch out for the unhinged. The "Son of Sam" began terrorizing Manhattan with random mass murders in 1977. Newspapers speculated, "He is probably an artist or creative type." After that, we only let expected visitors enter our office. The receptionist used the peephole to first check everyone out.

One morning our answering machine had a frightful threat on it. The voice ranted on in the murderer's fanatical style of jargon and ended, "This is the Son of Sam. You're next." It was an all-female office, and this terrifying situation went on for many weeks. The real criminal was finally apprehended in August 1977, and we were not attacked. We dodged that bullet. It was a relief to learn he was not a freelance artist or writer.

No business in a large city is secure from thieves and psychotics. At my first office on Madison Avenue, I encountered a tall, well-dressed man in a leather coat looking behind my desk with an empty box in his hands. In my alarm, I reacted like a scolding parent, dragged him by the sleeve to the front desk and complained to the receptionist for letting him wander into the offices without announcement. Quickly recovering from his surprise, he began cursing and threatening, pulled away and disappeared into the elevator. I kept pepper spray in my desk for many years after that.

Technology changes and employee turnovers are inevitable. The challenge is how to regroup and minimize damage. Changing personnel meant losing any candidate records that were not well documented.

In an effort to gain control and protect my records through standardization, I gladly embraced the early computer. Always enjoying technology and science, I was quick to jump on new innovations without realizing the short shelf life. Changes began moving at an unheard rate with the technology revolution.

The first computer system was a simple keyboard in my 58th Street office, attached by a phone line to an enormous mainframe computer in another office location. The salesman said they would provide a two-week training program with ongoing phone support. While portrayed as easy-to-learn, it took about two years to get fully implemented. By that time, the individual personal computer had come on the market. I also purchased an early roll fax device, but as it became useful, that too became outdated and changed to a plain paper copier.

Technology promised solutions to inevitable changes of staff and inadequate records. Several wonderful staff women left to get married—and then came the Barbara debacle. I had been fortunate to have very bright, responsible assistants and placement directors for the freelance area, but much of their knowledge was lost when they left employment.

The placement director position required a combination of creative taste, skill terminology and administrative background. I often took the time to train them as my assistant until they grew to manage the position by themselves. They were appreciative and stayed in a job they enjoyed until married. After my first two assistants, Robin and Donna married, I hired Babs. Babs sensed that a phone call at the end of the day was a hot account lead, so stayed late to fill the complex request for strike replacements. The newspaper labor union strike became a cash bonanza for our company. After two years, Babs also left to get married and was replaced by Maureen, a spirited redhead who lasted about five years until she got married. The reception desk remained a revolving training ground for employees, friends and family.

Most profits went back into the company as it grew to six people. Despite hurdles, the core business of "Creative Freelancers" continued to grow and be the primary source in town for placing freelancers.

Although staff often worked voluntarily through lunch and evening hours, late hours were never required. Allowing a lot of freedom and setting an example generally brought reliability. Employees frequently stayed for many years.

Employee changes always meant more work for me, so I tried to keep everyone happy in their job. I hesitated to fire salespeople who didn't produce.

Never underestimate competition. My competitors were nasty. Staff members told me they were asked to lunch, and offers were made but rejected. My employees said, "There is a good chance our competitor might just drain their knowledge and then dismiss them from the position."

By the end of the seventies, women in business were becoming a hot new topic. Eastern Airlines featured my picture with a story titled "A Creative Woman and A Unique Service" on the front page of their in-flight flyer. Soon afterward, I appeared in a television panel of three women entrepreneurs. The Channel 11 program was titled "Women in Business."

One of the panelists was Lillian Vernon, an early innovator of catalog sales.

When the notice date of a Sales Tax audit arrived, it seemed a traditional audit. We were obeying all the laws, so there was no reason for concern. I was not worried. However, it soon became evident that New York State had started interpreting the tax law differently from the guidelines established by my accountant. Although not the accounting practice of the times, freelance on-site professional labor was a gray area that suddenly became taxable.

We were caught off-guard. There were many different working situations lumped into our one accounting system, and we had not charged sales tax or collected resale certificates on the advice of my accountant. The audit became a nightmare, and I was entirely unprepared for the required changes. The government made "Creative Freelancers" the example for the freelance industry and demanded three years of retroactive taxes on everything. We seemed to be the first audit on their list, but other related industries soon followed.

Out of frustration, I wrote to all the NYS congressmen stating, "I represent several thousand freelancers who will be affected by this new interpretation." To my happy surprise, numerous representatives and senators responded, including several who were willing to propose legislation. A few thousand votes from freelancers evidently counted. Freelancers were becoming a recognized economic voting bloc.

The story was written up in the *New York Times* money column. As a result, the AIGA (American Institute of Graphic Artists) contacted me.

Some of the AIGA's members were also being audited, so they formed a group to fight and asked me to join them. While the larger lobby group had the illusion of being the more powerful, I would have been better off fighting for a single, simple freelancer exemption. Packaging firms, printers and freelancers all had different concerns, so various industry-specific issues bogged down agreements and action. It was a year of meetings and discussions that didn't solve the problem.

I stepped down from running the tax meetings, and the person who took over my job let the coalition fall apart. We all lost. Fortunately, or probably because of my congressional noise over the situation, the state gave my company a personal back tax exemption. The storm was over. The industry moved forward on a fair playing field now that the law was made clear. If the government wants more taxes, they will usually succeed, but going back three years to collect without acknowledging existing industry standards is a nasty money-making trick.

I knew balancing motherhood with business would be challenging but I was self-confident and elated by my first pregnancy. Dorothy, the part-time bookkeeper, organized a surprise baby shower.

Fortunately, I didn't have any morning sickness interruptions, and everything proceeded in my regular schedule until the last month when I felt like a beached whale. I probably did too much when I moved boxes and played tennis, as there were some birth complications. Nevertheless, Liz was born a healthy and fun extrovert like her father.

The drawback was Liz demanded constant attention and wouldn't sleep through the night for many months. The first six months were particularly arduous—as both office and baby battled for attention. Then I got better home childcare.

Chapter 17

Having it All

I wanted to have it all and thought I was Superwoman, but sleep and time were in short supply. One Monday morning, while juggling babies and business, I arrived at the office with my dress on backwards.

Mondays were particularly onerous. I was sleep-deprived from baby duty while my babysitter stayed with her daughter on weekends in another town. Working moms need reliable support systems and often challenge their mental and physical abilities with balancing family and business obligations. Motherhood was a mixture of joy and exhaustion.

I was "having it all"—a woman with family and business. However, the universe kept throwing additional unexpected asteroids my way, creating new impediments beyond the essential responsibilities.

During the first three years of marriage, the deaths of my mother, Rob's ex-wife, and both of his parents, seemed to be cosmic events that had massive emotional and financial impacts. Adding three stepdaughters into my orbit of responsibilities also seemed to come out of the cosmos. My world was changing rapidly with unexpected impediments.

It was the third year of my marriage when I became pregnant with Liz. Rob was in agreement to have a child. However, stressed out by the thought of my pregnancy, he took a sailing trip in the Caribbean without my consent. After too many drinks, he jumped off the boat and landed on a sea urchin. Rather than carefully picking the spines out of his hand, he just used a rock to crush what he couldn't get out quickly. It triggered a host of allergies. Anything made with dairy, mayo, wine, cheese, eggs, yeast, mushrooms, and small-boned fish caused him to break out in hives. I had to constantly worry about his diet and adapt our meals.

My needs during pregnancy were quickly dismissed. Pregnant women are rumored to get food pampering and should be expected to have mood swings. In this case, Rob was the moody one, getting my catered meals for his needs. I was expected to endure conversations about his host of allergies and business problems but not discuss my business issues, family concerns or the pending baby. His powerful voice just overrode what he didn't want to talk about. I frequently felt like a picture on the wall.

I never once got an ounce of sympathy, and my business was ceaselessly demanding. Stoically, I made myself tough it out, never missing a day of work and moving boxes at the office. With vigorous confidence, I stayed determined to do it all.

"My back hurt sitting in those hard chairs," he lamented, expecting me to sympathize after one Lamaze class. He refused to attend the other sessions, so I was the only woman without a husband. I needed a compassionate partner but had a fair-weather husband instead. His self-centeredness felt insurmountable. I took on his family and was going through my pregnancy stoically, but he couldn't give me a few hours! The romantic illusion ended with his refusal to attend the Lamaze class. I didn't see how I could last a lifetime in a marriage with this anger in my heart, but I would have to stick it out a while longer to have a second child. Age 36 was too old to start again and find another mate for my children. I resolved to be strong and not complain.

Rob was out in the Hamptons vacationing when my water broke two weeks early. He returned, but we had to finish watching his ball game on the TV before leaving for the hospital. I never went into labor. Since it was before the due date, my body wasn't ready, causing a Cesarean delivery. My doctor said that the weakness causing the break could occur in anyone, but I thought the likely reason was too much stress and physical exhaustion over many months. I felt unstoppable but was stopped by nature. Maybe I should not have played in a tennis tournament during my seventh month or moved office boxes. Reality was crashing down. The nurse comfortingly said that I had a good doctor. "He's quick and neat." Liz was born.

Several days after the delivery, post-partum depression set in. Major hormonal changes were going on inside my body, and a lot of stress was buried inside. A nurse prodded me to move more, and it hurt, so I broke down in uncontrollable sobbing. The cry lasted for two hours. No one could stop or comfort me. Finally, I was drained. They assigned a different nurse.

While spared labor, the month of disability and recovery that followed the surgery was restricting. I worked over the phone as much as possible. After five weeks, I was back at the office full-time. I envied women who had maternity leave and a comforting husband. Every bit of help that I had, I paid for. There were no family support systems, grandparents or relatives for assistance.

"You have a feisty one here," said my first baby nurse judiciously when just home from the hospital. Liz was a pretty baby with a full head of dark hair and lots of energy. She refused to nurse for the first month, perhaps because of the early birth. The second month, her appetite came in, and it became insatiable.

Liz grabbed you with her eyes and wanted complete eye contact. I looked for signs that she had the same early awareness that I had felt. While babies can express intense curiosity with their eyes, it is impossible to know what they are thinking.

Cute when awake, she knew how to charm, but Liz was an attention-demanding baby. Moreover, she was a light sleeper. I needed a whole night's sleep to function at the office, but Liz would wake up at one and a half hour intervals during the night and then stay awake for an hour each time. I could set my watch by it. After she returned to sleep, it took a while for me to drift into slumber, only to be re-awakened by her screams.

Gwen, the first nanny, let Liz sleep days whenever possible to avoid her daytime cries for amusement. Consequently, the baby was less tired at night. During the week, I often woke up to her nighttime noise and then dealt with her sleeping habits by myself all weekend.

At three months, the doctor said to limit her food intake. That was not easy. Liz was all about food and getting attention. If not played with constantly or fed, she howled. I was told by a consoling doctor, "It is good to have a child with a strong personality. They will be interesting adults."

Children expect a lot from their mothers. If I dared go out for an evening and leave Liz with the nanny, she felt rejected and would turn her head from me in anger for a whole day. Rob could get away with just showing up occasionally. Liz always smiled and giggled at the sight of him. She was definitely capable of detecting men, constantly reacting favorably to them and clearly having an early, active mind.

For one hour on Saturday, Rob would take her in the carriage for a walk to the park and then felt he had done his part. He fumbled clumsily when given a diaper to change, so was never asked. He joked that he would just stick the baby with a pin to get out of changing diapers before disposable diapers.

His attitude might have been acceptable when the man was the breadwinner, but I paid for hefty expenses, including childcare and family medical bills. Raising a family in Manhattan was primarily my overhead. Making the best of the situation, I resigned myself to Rob's selfish ways and just tried to enjoy the good moments. He still provided some laughs.

As I look back at the memorable moments in my life, family traditions and holidays created fun times of reunion and companionship. We held Liz's christening on Thanksgiving weekend so the girls would be home from school, and Ginny, the baby cousin I rarely saw, could join us. I hadn't seen Ginny or her husband since their wedding seven years before. My dad attended the christening and dinner at the apartment afterward. Rob selected a man his age as the godfather, and I chose a childless girlfriend as godmother. It was a rare time for all to be together.

In December, Gwen told me she was quitting because the baby was too much for her to handle. The good news was she had found an excellent replacement. She introduced Vi as someone who "could handle any baby."

From the first day, Vi proved a pro. She was a heavyset, 5' 10" Jamaican woman who took Liz out for long walks in the carriage all day. Vi walked all over the streets of Manhattan, no matter what the weather. Her theory was that if a baby could sleep through the noise of city traffic, she was exhausted. Otherwise, the carriage motion and passing scenes were entertaining, and the baby wouldn't cry. It worked! After a week, Liz began sleeping until 5 a.m.—an improvement, but still early for me. Vi would go home on Fridays at 6 p.m., and my weekend off was 24-hour childcare duty. Sleeping until 7 a.m. finally happened at 11 months.

Vi was an amazing survivor. She had raised four children by herself after her husband died. She had only a third-grade education but put all her children through college on her domestic care wages. Sadly, her grown children were embarrassed by her lack of education and made her feel unwanted in their social gatherings. She hadn't even been invited to her son's wedding. On weekends, she lived with a single daughter and grandchild for rent payment. Vi could be strict with other people's children, but she had spoiled her own.

Words like "kingdom" were a struggle for her to read in storybooks. It was difficult for her to understand that a balanced diet was needed. She mainly ate starch and sugar because meat products were scarce and expensive in her Jamaican childhood. I had to buy a five-pound bag of sugar for her every other week. The kids and I always remember the way she would chew on chicken bones to suck all the marrow out for nourishment. However, her steady, loving care and my dietary oversight were an early childhood winning combination, and she stayed for six years.

Rob usually didn't arrive home on weekday evenings until the children were in bed and almost asleep. Then he would stir them up with a greeting for a few minutes. When they were finally sleeping again, I would escape into the bathroom, and then close the door to sit reading a magazine for some private space and relaxation. Otherwise, he constantly interrupted me with his comments and needs.

While a non-smoker for seven years of marriage and promising he would never start again when we married, Rob began smoking horrible little cigars after five years. I complained and insisted he not smoke in the apartment, so he smoked on the building's staircase, but the odor drifted in and clung to his clothes.

Rob and I rarely argued because it was impossible to win over his powerful voice. I tried to laugh off any stress, but I wanted at least love and consideration for my efforts. He lived in the dream that he would make a lot of money again to make up for any current paucity. While I had fallen for it, I was losing conviction. Resentment kept building up with no release in sight.

It was shocking to learn that all Rob's earnings were spent quickly, and he didn't have any liquid assets. He assured me, "All businesses operate in debt." However, debt was totally alien to my common-sense nature and very troubling. Any disposable income went into entertainment, a quick stock tip going nowhere, or back into his business. I tried to convince myself that he knew what he was doing. Before marriage, I never contemplated that his outward success might be just a public image.

We disagreed about money matters, and it usually came to a head around tax time, when I would have to sign his return. I hated debt, but Rob saw bank loans using the beach house for collateral as an integral part of business and living. Although Rob's business was faltering, we both believed that would change.

We kept our income and finances separate from the beginning, with no clear agreements about the future. By default, I got all the new home expenses after marriage such as children, family medical and food bills. Rob continued to pay the rent on his bachelor pad where we lived, the beach house costs, entertainment, and his older daughters' expenses. There was never a joint banking account other than my father's marriage gift, which was spent on his beach house appliances.

It had also been assumed by Rob and others that he would inherit a sizeable amount of money from his parent's estate. They were wrong. The estate, divided between Rob and his two siblings, yielded about a year's living expenses—not the large fortune which was rumored. The money was used immediately because Rob was struggling to recover lost clients and wasn't taking his regular income.

Rob was a high-stake risk-taker who was talented and lucky early in life, but living on the edge doesn't always work out as anticipated. Now over fifty, his clients were retiring. Moreover, laws had changed, thwarting his ability to match low, competitive prices and attract new clients. Lucky breaks did not pick up again. He was becoming a dinosaur without modern technology knowledge. Fortunately, my business was growing, and I was getting excellent press write-ups, so I just kept playing the cards the best I could.

Finances play a crucial role in staying alive and maintaining peace. Marriage customs vary. "The man is king of his house" rule often runs into trouble with money-making women. A clear understanding of how financial and family responsibilities will be handled may be needed to replace the default. Be prepared.

It may be helpful to contemplate marriage as a business partnership. Before vows think, "How does each person compliment the other? How will tasks and expenses be shared? What are the long and short-term visions?"

Common goals and good exchange viewpoints are needed to succeed, and before a legal agreement is always the better time to bargain for outcomes. A big wave surfer understands that being truly prepared is needed to take on the huge swells when they happen.

Two years later, another baby was coming, my second child at age thirty-eight. As I searched for answers, the palm reader from my college boat voyage came to mind. Since the predictions of a late marriage and many children had transpired, I wondered if it might work again. Dorothy, my bookkeeper, heard that a mid-town restaurant's upscale bar had an excellent psychic, so she urged me to go.

The Monkey Bar was an intriguing spot, well-known for a number of historically significant events during its lifetime, including the untimely death of

Tennessee Williams, who mysteriously choked on an eyedropper. For decades, it had provided a cozy outpost for admen, after-hours politicians, and media barons looking for a bit of fun. I was about two months pregnant when Dorothy and I went over for lunch to meet the psychic.

After a greeting by the friendly, middle-aged woman, she led us to a corner table in the lounge. "Much of what I will say will be intuitive psychic ability, but Tarot cards are sometimes used as a guide."

I was disappointed that she was using cards. However, without giving the psychic my background, she turned over a few cards and said, "You will have a son." She didn't even know I was pregnant! As she turned over more cards, she saw conflicts and said there would be many lawyers in my life. Only a possible divorce lawyer seemed relevant.

Then she shocked me by saying, "You will live happily out of the city, and there might be a second move later in life." This was not good news. I wanted to stay in New York and dreamed of owning a brownstone. My business was good, and it seemed almost within my grasp. A second move elsewhere was not wanted and unfathomable. She also confirmed some predictions from my earlier palm reading, including the after-age-sixty warning.

I left, wondering if I would have a son and what adventures might be next.

Chapter 18

Biz Is Booming

Sensational news! *ADWEEK Magazine* of New York is sending a reporter to interview me for their feature story on the "Dynamic Dozen." The advertising industry's major weekly trade magazine had me highlighted as one of the top twelve women in advertising, under the age of forty, most likely to succeed. In their May 1983 edition, I was first on the list. The other women were all single and without children. Smooth sailing seemed to be ahead.

Business and family were both thriving. The months before had involved an intense search for new office space leading to relocation on 45th Street. The entire ninth floor in an older building between Fifth Avenue and Avenue of the Americas was chosen. Previously a photography studio, the windows were blacked out, and the interior was an empty, unfinished area. The office makeover had to be built to fit our needs and required a significant gut renovation job replacing floors, walls and ceiling.

The baby's due date was mid-July. Squatter tenants wouldn't leave on schedule—delaying the project. A complicated eviction process by the landlord finally got them out in May. Then demolition and construction work commenced. Even on the original three-month schedule, the timing was tight. Very pregnant and uncomfortable, I drove the workers on, urging them to move quickly saying, "The birth could happen any day. We might not make it in time."

As soon as the carpet was laid, we moved in. Office doors and other finishing touches were added later. Just a few days before Ken was born, we unpacked and got everything operating. Fortunately, it was a natural birth this time, allowing my return to work after two weeks.

At the realtor's suggestion, I intended to sublet the better front street view area for a higher per-square-foot price. The money-making sublet would pay off the construction loan and eventually create a profit. The ten-year lease contained an escalation clause for "Creative Freelancers Inc.," gradually increasing the rent over the term.

The next focus was to find a tenant for the front area sublet. It happened quickly. A small company with a one-year lease moved in. A sizable architect's firm signed a nine-year lease for the remaining time. The plan to cover costs worked seamlessly.

Business cruised along smoothly, occasionally interrupted by churning events. One November Friday afternoon, an unexpected lightning bolt hit our ship. Detained on a business lunch, I telephoned the staff. No one answered. Returning quickly, I found a note tacked on the door with a phone number. "There was a burglary, and we're all down at the police station." Apparently, a man was admitted for an appointment and began filling out an application for work. After checking out the office situation, he grabbed Elaine, the placement director, who was only 5'2", and held a man's shaving razor to her throat. Threatening to cut her throat, he proceeded to rob everyone, taking their money and jewelry. He didn't get much, so he impatiently demanded more.

"Where is Marilyn Howard, the name on the wall? She must have more money."

When the thief was told, "She's out to lunch," he responded by locking everyone into a back office and cutting that office phone line to await my return. The freelancers, who stopped by to pick up their Friday paychecks, were robbed as they entered and added to the back office prisoners.

This went on for two terrifying hours. During that time, the thief scouted all the rooms and piled up anything of interest by the front door. It was a month before the holiday season, so newly-purchased items were found, including a couple of new glass bowls. He took the bowls from their boxes to examine, covering them with his fingerprints. Finally, an entering freelancer saw another person being robbed, so he dashed back out into the hallway. The burglar chased him, and the office door slammed shut, locking them both outside. The elevator opened, and the game was up. The villain quickly disappeared into the crowd.

The office staff was understandably upset by the event. At the station, the police gave them books of mug shots and told to pick out the thief. Positively identifying anyone from a small mug shot in a book of thousands was unreasonable but mandatory. The women narrowed it down to two suspects, but that wasn't sufficient. The police wanted them all to swear to one person, or they wouldn't look for the person.

Logic would say to check the two photos against the fingerprints on the glass bowls, but they refused. Without a single, sworn positive identification from the entire group, they wouldn't compare fingerprints or bring anyone into a line-up. The law seemed to protect the criminal rather than the victims.

Since no one had been seriously injured, we were told that a potential murderer wasn't worth catching. He would get out very quickly and might return for vengeance. In fact, the intruder must have anticipated this happening. He had taken Elaine's wallet and identification, threatening that he would come to her home to get her if he was reported to the police. Of course, Elaine was terrified. She was a single woman living alone in a New Jersey house. I paid for the installation of an alarm system at her home and the monthly service charges until she left my employment about eight years later.

The police took the thief's pile of stolen items, left by the door in a large plastic bag. The anticipated evidence of fingerprint analysis never happened, and it was difficult to get the confiscated possessions returned. First, I had to go to Police Plaza in lower Manhattan for a release card and then drive to a lot in Long Island City to stand in a short but very slow-moving line of other frustrated people. Finally, the items were returned covered with black dust in a garbage bag. The glass bowls could not be returned to the store or given as holiday gifts.

Until that incident, the office was composed of only female employees. Thinking it might be a deterrent to thieves, I decided to hire a man for the open sales position. Mike, a prior art representative, was first man, but he didn't bring in any business and lasted less than a year. Then Bob, a previous studio manager, came aboard.

During Bob's first week, he appeared in my office with a flow chart documenting the pecking order of the six women and him. He wanted to know who he had to answer to. This was definitely a man-thing and not my management style. I was in charge, and the sense of purpose drove us all forward. We all just pitched in to get the job done. Many men think of business as power levels to which they answer and aspire, or in sports terms. Men employees were a new learning curve. One man hired later had the audacity to make passes at the women he interviewed, so he was quickly fired.

The first threatening hurricane wave rolled to shore slowly. In 1983, I received an Unemployment Insurance claim notice for a freelancer who had worked at one of our clients two days a week for four weeks. When the assignment was over, she got sick and was no longer available. Out of money several months later, she responded to a government advertisement, and they suggested she try to collect Unemployment Insurance. She was a professional college graduate who had signed a contract, so she didn't feel eligible. Nevertheless, they persuaded her to file a claim anyway.

I could have easily paid for the claim from my staff's unemployment insurance fund, but my lawyer and accountant advised against it. They said, "It will open a Pandora's Box, establishing the precedent that all freelancers are employees and not independent contractors." Making freelancers into employees would mandate much more than Unemployment Insurance. Full government employee benefits would have to be paid and taxes withheld by my company. In addition, we would have to factor the money and await payment from clients, while freelancers were paid weekly.

If it became a payroll, 30% more money would be needed from somewhere to cover the costs. Being the first to raise prices in a small competitive business could be suicide. Sending out lower-priced inferior talent was not an option—as it would ruin our business reputation.

It seemed prudent to fight the claim and follow the professional advice of the lawyer who wrote my company's contract terms. Presumably, it would be an easy win because it was the industry standard. Every place that I had ever worked or heard of in the industry paid freelancers as independent contractors.

At the hearing, I was greeted by an arbitrator who asked, "What is your position?" When learning I was the employer, he shocked me by commenting, "Well, we know who is going to lose this case." His mind was clearly prejudiced. The hearing proceeded, and we lost. Moreover, the court added an estimated assessment for three years of retroactive taxes. The tax amount would put our company out of business. After being found guilty of this uncommitted crime, my fight became the case of David against Goliath.

Our freelancers didn't have taxes deducted and were on a signed contract confirming they were independent contractors. They knew what the customer was paying and our flat, clearly-defined commission. None complained. They were all professionals who were happy with a higher net pay arrangement and receiving a 1099 form at the end-of-year.

The government had a list of questions and a vague rule for deciding independent contractors. Their list of questions was added to our enrollment papers and included: "Who has direction and control over your work?" "Do you supply your own tools?" "Are you a registered business entity?" and "Can you supply three clients of your own?" We embarked on differentiating the freelancers in our books, while searching for a better attorney. The general idea was "If it looks like a duck and walks like a duck, it is a duck."

The sharks were circling. Clear thinking was needed. I consulted with a top-rated employment lawyer who made an incredible discovery. The incompetent government employees had lost all the earlier hearing transcripts. It was a lucky break! There would now be a second chance with a better lawyer to prepare a new transcript. It also gave me time to think. A new, out-of-the-box business plan was needed.

Bob, my salesman, suggested an idea to reposition the business as an in-house production studio. Instead of just outsourcing, we would supervise projects, justifying a higher mark-up. It would utilize the freelancers while making more from their services. However, I was his only successful sale. He sold me some expensive equipment and never brought in any accounts.

Effective, self-motivated salespeople are a rare breed. Bob meant well, but I gave him too much freedom for too long. He never produced sales, and his salary was an unneeded expense. I learned that it's best to set specific sales goals within a timeframe and end the job if not a proven success.

Employees can be full of surprises. One day, I was in the hall outside Dorothy's office discussing a serious issue with a man whose voice was heavy. My bookkeeper came out of her office saying, "Please be quiet. I can't concentrate."

I replied, "Our conversation is important, so please be patient." The next day, she quit her job because I dared to refuse her. After being treated well for almost ten years, she had gotten spoiled and expected everything her way. I said leaving was her choice, but I paid the salaries and had rights in my own office. It was her loss. I subsequently hired Hilde, another very capable bookkeeper who was with me for over twelve years.

Some employees were passionate about their job. It was a business where they could make a difference by helping people find work. I did not micromanage and appreciated responsible people who didn't require supervision. The primary goal was to have a mostly self-functioning office that would provide me with income and time off for my family. However, my energies were spread too thin. I focused too much on administration and computers, with insufficient emphasis on client relationships. Living in a mixed reality can be confusing, even for skillful multi-taskers.

"Creative Freelancers" had a lot of potential for more growth. The name was a huge umbrella covering a multitude of consultants. We represented skilled talent and were experts at putting out fires in a lot of departments. Our primary emphasis was on designers, art directors, copywriters, illustrators, textbook editors, and production artists. It was a niche client base, with rare assignments from the general consumer market. The firm's customers were established publishers, advertising agencies, design studios, and corporations with creative departments. Unlike consumer-oriented businesses, which have an expanding group of markets and changing customer base, business-to-business is more limited, expands more slowly and has specialized needs.

When a new competitor launched an extensive advertising splash, we still remained the industry's gold standard. I was overconfident in our past reputation and didn't see the ominous threats on the horizon. Slow to catch warning signs, I began realizing we had a problem when several satisfied customers listed in our promotional brochure told us they had been approached by our competitor. Another way that competitors would find our contacts was by soliciting names from our freelancers or staff and following up with a sales pitch to our customers.

To combat competitors trying to dilute our success, I assembled a mailing promotion with the help of Larry, a brilliant advertising copywriter. Larry had been successful on several of our large advertising agency assignments. His work was rated as outstanding. He first appeared in my office for an interview at our 58th Street location. My stepdaughter was working at my reception desk and began dating him. She had general negative comments when they broke up, but omitted one central point. I was about to discover what it was.

Late one afternoon, Larry arrived in my 45th Street office, completely broke and without a place to sleep. He claimed his girlfriend had taken his money and thrown him out, so he would have to sleep on the street. Confused and wanting to help, I said he could use the office couch for the night. When we arrived the following morning, the furniture was all rearranged, little incoherent notes were all over the place, and Larry was nowhere to be found. When he finally arrived, he was a mess with his business shirt unbuttoned and half pulled out of his pants. Confronted, he admitted to taking the drug Percocet and added, "The doctor advances me prescriptions even when I don't have money because of my past repayment history."

As he came off the high, I tried to talk some sense into him and heard about problems festering below the surface for many years. At age thirteen, his mother had committed suicide. His talents pushed him into fast living with easy money as a teenager, leading to an 18-year-old son from an early marriage. When confronted, he acknowledged repeating his mother's pattern and slowly killing himself, so he agreed to go for treatment.

Without medical insurance, that was not easy. After many phone calls, I finally found a place in Harlem that would take him and then gave $50 to his ex-girlfriend to bring him in for treatments the next day. Surprisingly it worked, and he later moved out to Long Island for a new life. For several years, he occasionally called to tell me about his job working at a rehabilitation center helping others, but then the calls stopped.

Our freelancers were a hard-working, industrious group. We treated everyone with respect and invited those who worked with us during the year to our holiday party. The festive evening was always an enormous success, which helped build loyalty. Freelancers spread the good word about our services and were our public advocates. As the business and reputation grew, the top of the mountain was within sight.

Chapter 19

Supermom

Still angry and hurt from Rob's refusal to attend the Lamaze class, I asked my earlier roommate, Sandra, to be my Lamaze coach for Ken's birth three years later. She accompanied me at all the meetings and was a dependable, supportive friend.

A search for an experienced doctor willing to try a natural birth after the previous Cesarean delivery had been successful. Most didn't want the liabilities of possible scar rupture. On schedule, my water broke in the morning, so I took a cab to the hospital by myself. The labor was minimal throughout the day. I notified Sandra, and she arrived. Around six p.m. the doctor went out to dinner after giving me a stimulant— expecting it to be a long night. A half-hour later, labor suddenly started in earnest.

The nurses kept urging a Lamaze breathing technique to delay the birth. However, it was impossible to stop Ken's delivery, which happened an hour and a half later. The floor doctor was ready. My physician had been paged from dinner, but he didn't arrive until the last minute. Still dressed in his suit jacket, he entered the room just in time for the delivery. Two pushes later—without any anesthetic—Ken was born. When asked if I wanted my husband in the delivery room, I replied with an emphatic, "No. All he knows how to do is crack jokes."

Ken was an easy baby who slept through the night after a few weeks. It would have been less stressful, if he had been my first child. Unfortunately, by the time he was born, Liz was a very active three years old. There was no rest, and I returned to work full-time after two weeks.

Liz had sensed competition coming. When I was describing to her how babies are in a mommy's tummy, she leaned over and bit my pregnant stomach, leaving teeth marks that lasted for days. However, Liz loved her new baby brother after he was born and was very protective. She actually got to see more of me for the first two weeks, rather than less, as I was usually away at work. On one of the first days, she came running into my room excitedly saying, "Come quickly!" Dragging me by the hand, she approached the crib and eagerly said to her brother, "I brought dinner, Kenny..."

Watching *Gone with the Wind* inspired the choice of Ashley as Ken's middle name. Ashley is a compassionate character who knows how to love a woman in the story. I wished I had married a considerate man like that instead of a tough alpha male, so I gave the name to Ken. At the time, it was primarily a man's name, but that same year, Ashley suddenly became a popular as a girl's name. Ken was never thrilled with his middle name.

Rob's best contribution to our family was finding a wonderful godfather. Since Rob was fifty-five at

Ken's birth, he realized a boy needed a younger father image and a man to be there if anything should happen to him. His contemporaries were too old, and his pick of an aging godfather for Liz was just a trophy title. Becky and Dougal were friends from the Hamptons. Rob made the appeal, and Dougal accepted, taking the relationship seriously and becoming a wonderful part of our family ever after.

Dougal, a kind, quintessential Scottish gentleman, managed the U.S. division of a Scottish fabric company—importing fine fabrics for high-quality men's suits and decorating. Becky, his wife, was a successful oil trader. Becky and I were both supermoms who ran businesses and shared laughs while juggling offices, children and au pairs. We would laugh about how we could successfully make many business decisions, but deciding which pizza to order with the kids was always a struggle.

The two childless girlfriends picked as godmothers were not as successful in the roles. The christening was the last time either saw their godchild. I could have chosen other people but thought they would enjoy a child in their lives. One honestly told me that it hurt her too much because she couldn't have children of her own. The other godmother just faded away without giving a reason. They probably didn't realize their conflicted feelings until later.

Our two-bedroom Sutton Place apartment was comfortable for two people, but a family of four plus the nanny and visiting stepdaughters packed us in like cattle. To add a third bedroom and storage, I designed a wall of cabinets to fit along one end of our large living room and hired a carpenter to build it. The wall could be separated into individual pieces of furniture for a future location, wherever that might be. The new small bedroom held Vi with the baby.

When the older daughters came for a visit, they slept in the living room until both children could sleep together in the second bedroom and Vi was gone for the weekend. Only Allie lived with us for an extended period while attending drama classes and auditioning for acting roles.

My father, Laura and Allie would usually join our foursome on the big holidays. We wandered Fifth Avenue to see the "Easter Parade" of ladies showing off their Easter bonnets after Easter brunch. The stroll led past a group of horse-drawn carriages into Central Park's miles of greenery surrounded by the tall skyscrapers of Manhattan. The children loved to watch the men and boys maneuvering their remote-controlled sailboats in the pond as the adults chatted on the benches. Our preferred park exit led past the seals in the ever-entertaining zoo.

At Christmas, we strolled down Fifth Avenue again, but this time checking out the holiday decorations. Cleverly-animated figurines moving around the Saks Department Store windows caught everyone's attention and had a waiting line of viewers. Across the street was the gigantic Christmas tree at Rockefeller Center with outdoor ice skating below.

On the way home, the FAO Schwartz toy store provided fun and excitement. We lost Ken inside the store one year, but found him sound asleep in a giant, stuffed gorilla's arms.

Kenny liked to hide in unexpected places, sometimes causing consternation. He was quick to get away when I turned my head, only to be found hiding behind a vending machine or in a rack of clothes. The scariest disappearance was during the Thanksgiving Day Parade. We were perched on our usual hill at the bottom of Central Park West, near the start of the parade. As we stared at the enormous parade balloons, Ken was suddenly gone. I stayed with Liz while Rob ran around looking. He found Ken safely standing by Walter Cronkite, the famous news reporter. Ken said he knew where he was.

No place is safe, and parents must always be vigilant. Kenny was an adorable, active little boy with a crop of light blond hair. A man approached his stroller in a hardware store saying, "What a cute little boy. If I was going to kidnap someone, it would be him." It was a very creepy thing to say.

On another occasion, I had Kenny in the stroller with Liz walking next to me at the small mall of shops and restaurants inside the Citicorp building. A strange man came up to Kenny with compliments and started playing with him. I didn't stop and learned later that kidnappers often worked in teams. One distracts the parent while the other child is lured away.

Rob's older daughters had scars from a tumultuous early life. Their mother's alcoholism at first made them very cautious with alcohol. However, Allie, the youngest, started drinking too much in her late twenties. She met and developed a relationship with Gary, an intelligent guy with serious problems. Gary's father, a professor at Harvard, had exerted a lot of pressure on him at an early age to be a high achiever. Unable or unwilling to measure up to family expectations, Gary started drinking in the morning before high school and later moved on to drugs. He sounded like a professor when sober, but he could never stay sober for long. Allie refused his marriage proposal—even when pregnant.

Gary's father cared about the family. He let the two of them move their family into his beach house on Martha's Vineyard, hoping his son would lead a sober life. The Vineyard was supposedly a "dry" island, where liquor could only be purchased in restaurants. Allie stayed dry, but Gary found a way.

Laura, the oldest, went through a difficult time when her mother first died, but with time and therapy, she returned to her naturally vivacious, extroverted personality. She adapted to new computer skills as they took over the graphic arts industry and was steadily employed as a visual artist in Boston for many years. Compassionately, Laura helped feed the poor each Thanksgiving. While she had several long-term relationships, Mr. Right has eluded her life.

After her mother died, Rob's middle daughter, Jennifer left school and moved to Oregon. We didn't see her for several years. Her buried anger and baggage from childhood seemed to engender clashes with her sisters and father, but she had a very soft side. Jennifer returned for a visit several years later and stayed in our living room. I had a horrible case of the "swine flu," and she pitched right in taking care of Liz without being asked. I had a lot of respect for Jennifer's sense of responsibility, and we bonded. After she returned to the west coast, we corresponded frequently, but I didn't see her again for many years.

Little Liz grew to have a powerful voice and her father's outgoing personality. All the doormen on Sutton Place knew her. She would walk up to them and chatter about anything on her mind. Sometimes she just made noise or sang loudly to get attention and fill the air. Liz was a noisy but charming extrovert.

She seemed a born saleswoman. Even a slide lock on the kitchen door didn't stop her persistent sales pitch for something to eat. If she knew there was cake in the refrigerator, she was relentless. After a half-hour of presenting every possible argument, she would take a short break and then launch into the tirade all over again, like she had never said it before. She left no stone unturned and persistently pursued her goal, just like her father.

Starting at a very early age, both children were enrolled for a few days a week in the United Nations International Preschool, a reasonably-priced school near the United Nations. All private schools in Manhattan had a long waiting list to get in. Anticipating a wait, I registered early and was surprised when Liz was taken at 13 months for one day a week.

Ken joined her when he was about two. The school was halfway to my office, so I walked them a mile to school in the morning with Ken in a stroller and then continued about another mile to work near Sixth Avenue. Vi picked them up.

There were times when I would leave for my office in the morning—guilt-ridden and exhausted. My children were crying in the background and begging me to stay when I got on the elevator. I rationalized that Vi was better equipped to raise my children. Evenings and weekends were all I could handle.

Manhattan sparkled in my eyes, even in bad weather. There were world-renowned historic sites, theater, museums, shopping, restaurant dining, bars, and clubs within easy reach.

My dress shoes were left at the office or kept in a bag while I traveled back and forth in sneakers. Undeterred by the climate, I charged through freezing winter winds and jumped slush puddles after snow. No inconvenience made me want to live anywhere else. It's hard to describe the excitement of going to work each day. Passing fascinating store windows and hurrying crowds made me feel in the center of the universe.

All the neighborhood mothers and nannies congregated in the corner park on 57th Street and the East River. It was a community meeting spot where we watched the children play on weekends. A lawyer friend from the park had a little boy named Peter, who was such a terror he was expelled from nursery school for biting other children. However, Liz and Peter played well together, so we struck a weekend deal.

After Vi left on Friday, both my children competed for my attention. It was chaos with them screaming, running around, pulling toys off the shelves and throwing stuff around. I arranged for Peter's mother to take Liz on Friday nights, and I took Peter on Sunday afternoons.

Ken calmed down after spending Friday night as my only child, so I could give Liz attention on Saturday. On Sundays, I hired an outside babysitter for Peter's visit, and I went to the Vertical Club for a sauna and exercise. Those three hours of relaxation at the club were often my only personal break in the week.

As they got a little older, a walk inside the Metropolitan Museum of Art on Saturday—joining museum tours when possible—was an enjoyable environment for the children as well as me. Liz changed into a more reasonable and controllable child when she approached the age of five. There is a reason that age is the start of kindergarten.

Despite their hefty costs, finding the right private school was a challenge because of a large demand from the upwardly mobile baby-boomers. Getting accepted was competitive. The public schools were poorly equipped and often dangerous. There were private school entrance exams and interviews for kindergarten. Luckily, Rob's older daughters had attended The Hewett School, so Liz was a legacy applicant and accepted. Soon after she entered, they had her tested for a learning disability. I was told she would need private tutors to manage her class work. The expenses kept climbing, our living conditions were claustrophobic, and my marriage was shallow. Pressure was building.

At the time of my marriage, I equated physical affection with emotional caring but learned they don't always go together. My father was not affectionate but was dependably there when needed. Rob was demonstratively affectionate and never hesitant to give a hug, but he was a fair-weather companion who wasn't there for my needs. He even went so far as to declare, "I don't care what you have to say." Conversations always revolved around Rob's business, friends and family, or politics and sports. He only listened to subjects that interested him, quickly changing the subject if not to his liking and forgetting what I said. It was rude and often hurtful.

Finally, in desperation, I suggested a marriage counselor, but he wouldn't participate. My body experienced overload and I needed someone who would provide at least emotional reinforcement, but there was no one.

For a while, I remained strong, but my wall of self-sufficiency was cracking. I felt used, unloved and trapped. There was a lot of pressure on my shoulders and no emotional or financial support. Our age difference added to the problems. He was at senior crisis time with a philosophy of "Eat, drink and be merry for tomorrow we die." I was at the nest-building stage of life and looked forward to a semi-normal married life with children.

Life always looks better from behind a smile and with enjoyable companions. It lightens the load of things that are not up to expectations. The Hamptons provided entertainment and camaraderie from May until the end of October. Everyone played with the children, and there were other women for conversation. Each evening at high tide, anyone interested in water skiing would appear on our deck for cocktails and skiing. Some stayed for dinner. I had the central role of planning and cooking, while Pam and the other women around made suggestions and pitched in on the work. They were fun evening with beautiful sunsets on the bay and laughter.

Hampton beach house life morphed into dinner parties and small group city activities in the winter. We often met friends or business associates at a restaurant for drinks or dinner. A friendly crowd was always dining at Rob's frequent hangout, Neary's Irish Pub, a block away. He had been their customer for many years and was treated well. Life with Rob created some fun and laughs, but I craved a compassionate partner and a home that we owned together.

In 1984, my dream was to own a multi-use, three story brownstone, with business and family under one roof. It would be a much easier commute to have my offices on the main floor and family with children living above.

To me, rent payments were wasted money, and the money would be better spent paying a tax-deductible mortgage on a home investment, which could grow with inflation. If we couldn't afford a townhouse, at least we should buy a more spacious apartment and build some equity. The beach house was a pre-marital asset in his name, and the Sutton Place apartment was also his lease and rental.

Our Sutton Place apartment was expected to turn co-op. A money-making announcement came in the mail. We would be receiving a legal document called the "Red Herring Prospectus"—a preliminary filing by a company with the SEC, presenting the company's initial public offering. It would describe the details of the offer and "insider price."

Traditionally, the building owners presented a low price to the renting residents in order to flip the building into a co-op. The new owners could sell to others at a higher price or remain as the co-op owner. After a limited timeframe, the option price would expire. If not accepted, the unit remained a rental apartment until the tenant died or left.

In Rob's case, his rent was fixed as "rent-stabilized" by New York, so his rent was lower than the proposed monthly charges. He didn't want to buy and planned to live there for the rest of his life.

I wanted to buy at the insider price and flip for profit to buy a larger family living space. Two active toddlers, babysitters and stepdaughters would be an unlivable condition for much longer. This was our opportunity.

Rob had previously owned a large co-op on Park Avenue with his first family. He experienced an economic downturn, so people who couldn't pay the charges left, leaving the remaining co-op owners with the added maintenance cost of abandoned apartments. He feared the New York real estate market was overvalued, and prices would fall again.

I saw Manhattan with exciting potential and had saved money for a home purchase. Rob wasn't interested, but I kept hoping he would change his mind

.

Chapter 20

Rethinking the Dream

Life has juggling acts of fire sticks and high wire walks. Complex business and family situations occurred at the same time in multiple arenas. In addition to office moves, trying to grow the business, and family activities, unexpected world events and legal issues competed for attention. There was never a dull moment, and the boredom of childhood was long gone.

The first challenge in business management is recognizing opportunity, and the second is maintaining the advantage. There is an obstacle race to the desired treasure. Both legal and financial mountains have to be climbed before the finish line.

As predicted, many lawyers entered my life. The unemployment insurance struggle began early in 1983 and became my Achilles heel for several years. It was time to rethink my business structure while preparing for the next court battle.

Looking for new paths around roadblocks and anticipating a potential change to our operations, the illustrators seemed a prime group to promote as independent contractors. I called Bernie, a charismatic art director from a large advertising agency who had come for an interview shortly before the previous office lease ended. He loved working with illustrators and was interested in full-time or freelance side jobs for an after-forty career. Advertising agencies preferred the under-forty age group, so planning a backup career was wise. If his art director job was lost in a slowdown, it would be challenging to reenter.

Bernie's engaging manner of asking relevant questions and then listening carefully made him stand out as someone who would be good at sales. He had a sense of humor, excellent people skills and empathy for other folks' problems. I remembered our conversations about illustration, so I asked if he might be interested in developing an illustration division. He accepted and became a top-notch selection.

Vic was hired for the design and staffing business. He was a distinguished middle-aged man with slightly gray hair—a perfect account executive type willing to make sales. However, his work schedule became compromised within months because his wife was diagnosed with cancer. Four children needed to get to school in New Jersey every day, so he didn't arrive until late morning or noon.

Hiring and firing can be more consequential than moving the monkey off the table. It can be devastating to lives. A woman's sensitivity is helpful in business, but managers have to make tough decisions. The manager deals the cards to others, and a problematic quandary is often "them or me?" Since business is about making money, a small business owner's family expenses have to be weighed against salaries. It is easy to spend income on them and difficult to make the business grow for me. I gave Vic a longer than ordinary advance notice but let him go. He appreciated the extra time and became a customer in later years.

Paul took over Vic's accounts and made sales calls. He was a friendly, young, energetic guy who didn't mind calling lists systematically. When Paul ran out of places to call, he asked for suggestions. Paul was also knowledgeable about computers and was instrumental in getting my first Apple Macintosh system. Time was never wasted, and new clients were opened up.

I looked toward technology as a way to control business operations. Employees changed, and their manual records were very inefficient. Bookkeeping and billing could be better handled by the computer. After using an early PC, the Apple computer was embraced to test graphic artists, plus perform all the database and accounting functions. Foolishly, an accounting software package was purchased first. It was complex and not adjustable to my business. A programmer was needed to customize a workable system as no matching software packages existed for my business at that time. Charting new territory always requires time-consuming, innovative thinking. Then the copycats come along and have it easier.

While the odds of winning are good when the cards are correctly in place, cards don't always line up neatly. Life is full of unexpected circumstances.

Rob's never saved for that inevitable "rainy day." His cash was spent quickly, leaving the beach house as his only asset. His style took high risks on hot tips without researching the leads thoroughly. However, he did have some useful hot tips that I carefully examined.

His first "hot" lead was to a computer chip manufacturer back in 1981. My attitude was if there was a 75% chance of winning, I would venture forward. I purchased the initial public offering on the stock at $7 per share. It went up to $70. My investment was multiplied ten times!

Then the stock started going down for no apparent reason. I wanted to sell but my first problem was the stock certificates were used as collateral for my office construction loan and at the bank. When I paid off the loan, my broker kept saying, "The decline is just temporary," and refused to sell. As the price kept descending, he kept refusing. Finally, Rob got on the phone and insisted the stock be sold. The broker responded to a powerful man's voice and sold at $12 per share. It was still a decent profit, but much less than the high. A valuable lesson was learned about how hype and fashion are intrinsic to market investments. This old motto is still wise, "When it doubles, sell half; when it triples, sell it all."

On Rob's second recommendation, he introduced an owner of real estate property being developed near the Hamptons. The money from my stock sale purchased the last lot at the development in Quogue, Long Island. After reviewing floor plans and talking with builders, I learned building on the lot for a house was a lot of work and not much profit for an inexperienced outsider. Moreover, a lot of construction issues could create big headaches. Hence, it stayed as a raw land investment until it became profitable.

The unemployment case of David against Goliath continued. The word "freelancers" seemed to conjure up free spirits skipping out on taxes to the government. In reality, we performed all government requirements dutifully, and filed 1099 forms on all the independent contractors, who might otherwise not have reported their income. Nonetheless, they pursued us like an enemy. My small business was an easier target to go after than larger companies with a staff of lawyers.

Fortunately, New York State had incompetently lost the first arbitrated hearing transcript, so we had the opportunity for a rerun. My new, high-powered attorney specializing in labor law warned, "The first level of arbitration is an incestuous system. It generally goes against the employer." He added, "The case will get better treatment when it goes up to the New York Court of Appeals in Albany. Getting the best possible hearing transcript to send to Albany is critical." Every plausible hearing question from the prosecution was carefully rehearsed. If I followed the script and just answered the questions, all the answers needed would be on recordings and transcripts.

The presentation became a dramatic movie spectacle. The government's appointed prosecution lawyer only asked one question. Then it was my lawyer's turn. In a clear and reasonable voice, he asked all the opposition's questions in the order and manner that he preferred. The freelancer, who had returned to her home state of California, was brought in via a phone conversation. She unequivocally confirmed our point of view: "Yes, I am an educated professional who knew all the terms and should not have been eligible to collect unemployment insurance. However, I wasn't going to turn down money if they wanted to give it to me."

The prosecutor was left speechless and without further questions—an unusual position for any attorney. "Congratulations on a case well done," he said to my lawyer, as no issues were left open. The transcript was airtight. If logic was to prevail, we should have won at this lower hearing level, but when the decision came in the mail, we had lost—as my lawyer had predicted.

The next stage involved an expensive, lengthy legal brief for presentation to a higher court in Albany, where the case would undergo verbal deliberation and produce a response. If the appeal was lost, New York State would claim an impossible payment of back taxes. The only answer would be closing my company.

Although confident that we would win if justice prevailed, "just in case," my lawyer advised moving my home and any assets out of New York State to securely preserve them. He said, "Unemployment insurance is an add-on tax paid by the employer and not a withholding tax taken from salaries, so they won't cross state boundaries to seize assets from the corporate officer." These were threatening clouds. I had to cover everything to weather a potential disaster.

"Tough luck!" should have been the words used in the verdict. The court's only answer to our multiple-point legal justification was "guilty," by using a newly-expanded definition of "direction and control" with no other factors from our legal brief considered.

Was The New York Court of Appeals just a "Kangaroo Court?" This case seemed a mockery of the principals for an unbiased trial. Their simple response was unfair and incredible but legal. Justice was not served, but the law was successfully expanded.

The sharks had their meal. The state was able to use the precedent from my small case to go after other businesses. At the very least, they should have taken industry standards into account and not imposed retroactive taxes. Instead, however, they whitewashed over the facts and established a three-year retroactive penalty on my ethical business. If the government wants to expand taxes, they will usually succeed. Neither reason nor lawyers will stop them.

In business and in life, we must accept what we can't change and change what we can, so that is what I proceeded to do.

Chapter 21

Realizing the Path

I opted for the only survival answer, which was cumbersome. Before any final invoice arrived, the original corporation was dissolved and replaced by two new corporations, one for management of independent contractors and the other, a temporary employment agency. Under the latest incarnations, I could sidestep the verdict because neither company would be a copy of the original and the original company no longer existed.

There was still the chance that they would attach the owner's assets, so I prepared to move my home and financial assets to Connecticut. The signposts had pointed. The direction was written on the wall. Just giving up to crash and burn was not an acceptable option.

Intense months followed. I didn't have the luxury of time to be angry. Too many things had to get done. I also didn't want to spoil the highs of owning a business and having children. Knowing that negative thoughts can begin a downhill cycle, I automatically responded to any ball that came my way, playing the game to the best of my ability.

I can see why businessmen frequently use analogies that relate to sports. To succeed, one has to hit hard, calculate the best play and go for it. It requires managing a team of unrelated, diverse people to win. Family management is very different. Being a mother involves sensitivity and nurturing. Sometimes those skills can be helpful in the office, but they can't dominate.

Switching between the two worlds was often therapeutic. After dealing with predicaments at the office, walking into a room of active children was entering a different reality. Office pressures decreased, replaced by the demands of motherhood. It unburdened existing office tensions to manage another list of high priorities. Although neither situation was relaxing, it was better than obsessing over a setback. Sometimes, sleep worked out answers, and concerns were resolved the next day.

Rob's business predicament worsened. His French government patron and main client for many years retired, while tough economic times and competitive bids thwarted new efforts. Potential clients were much younger, and voice mail made selling more difficult. Now in his late fifties, Rob was not readily part of the younger networking loop.

"You're great at sales, and your good luck at finding new accounts will happen again." Clint, his brother and partner, played to Rob's ego and urged him to make up the lost sales with new business. As the administrative partner, he fought against layoffs for his long-term employees—some of twenty years. In addition to sales calls, Rob courted prospective clients at restaurants and bars, thinking they might lead to profitable projects. Unfortunately, most new projects collapsed, and it would be on to the next "near-win."

Both brothers went through all their money, including their retirement funds, to pay the business overhead– a noble but impractical idea. Rob also took home equity money from the beach house for living costs. I knew he really believed in himself and I foolishly believed his hype about new leads that didn't turn into customers–while paying family bills without complaint and becoming an enabler. After losing all retirement savings, salaries had to end. Everyone lost.

In order to obtain cash to buy our apartment, which was going co-op, I had put the Quogue land up for sale. My lot had supposedly almost tripled in value, but no buyers were around for the asking price. Raw land is less liquid than homes because of fewer buyers. An offer finally came in from a real estate saleswoman at a very low price. Beaten down and hungry for the cash, I said okay on the phone. As luck would have it, I had another offer for my much higher asking price a few days later.

Contracts were not signed, so I assumed I could change the deal to my better offer. Not so. Apparently, a verbal acceptance was enough to make a legal deal in New York State at that time. Although this was my first real estate venture, nobody, including the broker, had advised me about the real estate law in New York. I offered a half commission to settle, but she wouldn't accept and wanted it all.

I could pay both commissions in full and still come out ahead with the price difference, so I went with the better offer and a court battle. In the end, the judge arbitrated the commission that I offered in the first place. It was a lot of additional aggravation for the same result.

Along with other savings and investments, I now had a sizeable down payment for our co-op. However, Rob refused to allow the purchase of his apartment, even though he didn't have to put any money down and would be a 50% owner. He didn't want to move anywhere, despite the cramped living conditions for everyone else.

I had saved and invested to purchase a home. There was no way I could continue to raise my children in that apartment. Then the court verdict arrived, putting my financial assets in a precarious legal position. As a final blow, Liz's test scores showed a learning disability. Raising children in Manhattan became even more expensive and complicated.

At the request of the school, a child psychologist produced an absorbing report by interviewing and testing Liz over a series of meetings. She rated poor at logical sequential subjects such as math but high on the verbal and abstract. There was an auditory weakness, which made her get distracted easily, resulting in poor classroom focus. Fortunately, she had a unique ability to overcome obstacles by restructuring tasks in her own fashion. They said it indicated strong survival skills. However, supplemental tutors would be needed for her learning disability. Small private schools were not equipped to deal with special circumstances.

I accepted the decision of the universe. Some mountains are too high to climb. My hope of owning a home in New York City was abandoned. The cost of living in New York outweighed my ability to live there without another breadwinner. Liz would need private tutors on top of private school costs. Ken's education in Manhattan was out of reach. I saw all my money going into expenses with no equity for the future.

Moreover, my assets were at risk in New York. I would move out of New York without him and get a divorce. The writing was on the wall, and my fate was sealed.

Chapter 22

Four Fateful Months

I played my final card by giving Rob the alternative of moving with me. He wouldn't move anywhere.

The court invoice would be arriving soon, and the best time for moving was at the end of the school year, so a new home was needed quickly. As I began searching, the suburban coastal communities of Connecticut were an attractive and reasonable commuting distance. In February, I made several trips to view properties.

The following months of March through June became four fateful months that changed my life, with gales intensely swirling around me. When the March winds began, I was sucked into a vortex of activity.

Pressured by time and money, my short window of time was a broker's dream. I viewed my eventual Greenwich condo during the first week of March–before it was advertised. The community was within the bus district for the elementary school and fit my other requirements. Three-bedroom condos with basement, attic and garage were hard to find in my price range, so I put in an immediate bid. That first Saturday in March, the deal was made.

As soon as the binder was signed, new sirens began going off. The next day, I received an emergency call from Claude, my office building's superintendent. The ceiling pipes had burst in the floor above my company, and water was gushing in through the ceiling. Claude turned the water off, but my arrival on Monday morning found a disastrous mess. Water had poured down on my computer, plus destroyed numerous ceiling tiles and files.

The insurance agent was reviewing the damages on Monday when another emergency call came from Jamaica Hospital. My eighty-six-year-old father had just been admitted with a heart attack. After the insurance agent left, I rushed to the hospital where he was sedated and resting quietly. The doctor said Dad had lost one-third of his heart capacity but would survive with proper treatment. Feeling better because he could talk and seemed okay, I returned to Manhattan, where my two small children and office calamities were awaiting attention.

Wednesday morning, a second distress call came from the hospital. Dad had pulled all the intravenous tubes and was insisting on going home. He had never been a patient in a hospital and didn't like it. In his day, you only went into a hospital to die, and he preferred to die at home.

I rushed out to the hospital again, to plead, beg and reason to no avail. Neither the doctor, staff psychiatrist, nor I could convince Dad to stay. He was wary that someone might try to sedate him, so he refused to eat or drink. It was futile. He had the right to leave and defiantly said, "If you don't take me home, I will take a cab." Reluctantly, the doctors provided his heart prescriptions—warning that they were not as effective as the intravenous medication. Although aware that he might kill himself by leaving the hospital, Dad just wanted out. As we drove home, he wistfully mused, "I guess I'm an old man now."

At home, his breathing was hoarse and labored. He could barely walk across the room. I called my brother, bluntly announcing that they should talk because Dad might be dead by morning. The scare tactic didn't work. Dad's attitude was nonchalant. I lay awake, listening to his arduous breathing throughout the night, wondering what to do. The next day I called a nursing service for someone to stay with him during the day. Then I rushed into the city for other screaming concerns, always arriving back in time to feed and take care of him in the evening. Thursday night was the same.

Finally, his friend and neighbor, Mr. Leonard, persuaded him to return to the hospital because he was a burden to his family. Always a very self-sufficient man, the last thing Dad wanted was to be a burden on anyone, so on Friday morning he acquiesced to return on Saturday to the hospital. My brother planned to arrive from Ohio Friday night and would escort him in the morning. Weakened from three days without intravenous medication, Dad died Saturday night after being admitted. He was my rock. A foundation stone was removed.

Pastor Hansley, the pastor from the church of my youth, described Dad very eloquently in his eulogy saying, "...listening to his son and daughter, I have a picture of a gentleman—a moral man—one who is convinced that there are values established for all time to be handed down from one generation to another. Values such as decency, truth, integrity, a man's word, industry, respect for law, the worth of human life as grounded in our religious tradition. Such values help to preserve a society fit for our children and our children's children.

"He was independent — didn't want to lean on anyone, wanted to carry his own pack—a self-made man. From orphan to engineer, he was a Horatio Alger story. Of course there is no such thing as a self-made man. But there are those who do more with what God has given them than others by application and hard work. As an orphan, he could have felt that the world owed him a living, but it was an excuse he didn't use.

"As Marilyn and Edson talked about their father and their contacts with him, including these last days, it became clear to me that although he had lost his wife ten years ago, he was not really alone. He had his children and grandchildren. He was very much cared about. How much that means—to know that there are those who care and are ready to express their caring in practical, helpful ways, even when it isn't easy to do that. And usually it isn't. Caring is demanding. We see this so clearly in our family relationships. It means giving up something of one's own life for the sake of another: parents for children, children for parents."

Dad overcame the odds after losing both parents and being left an orphan at sixteen. He refused to give up and followed his dream. Life was tough, and he learned to survive.

Death is always upsetting, even when someone is eighty-six and ready. Losing a close family member is like losing an arm. With crushing sadness, I moved forward. For the next two months, I was on automatic controls, mechanically maximizing the hours in every day without allowing myself to think.

My brother stayed for two weeks to help with the funeral and getting the house ready for sale, but then he returned to Ohio at the beginning of April, leaving me to finalize all the repairs, sell the house and file the estate taxes. There were piles of chores including house painting, children to be cared for, legal negotiations, and a business to manage. The Greenwich condo closing was at the end of March, and my move date was set for the end of June.

At the end of March, the separation agreement was also signed. My divorce attorney said that my potential for earning income and Rob's advancing age meant the state might make him my ward and responsibility, rather than the other way around. It was almost unbelievable, but I might owe him alimony and not get child support! Apparently, divorce judges try to avoid any potential expense to the state, so they usually pass the burden on when possible.

I didn't demand anything from Rob, so the settlement was quick, and I paid the small divorce fees. Rob offered a minimal child support payment plus our only marital asset of some land. The written separation agreement stated that the land was to be sold later for the children's college education. There was no question about custody of the children.

I visited Sandra, my earlier roommate and Lamaze coach, early in May. Her dearly-loved younger brother, my friend Wade, was celebrating his thirty-ninth birthday. I stopped by with some of Mrs. Field's chocolate chip cookies. Sandra had been taking care of him tirelessly for the past two years, ever since he had come down with a newly-discovered disease called

AIDS. Wade looked thinner and was in his bathrobe, but no other signs of sickness appeared. As we chatted in the living room, I tried to be cheerful and couldn't imagine the worst. He commented that he might not see his fortieth birthday, but I urged him to think positively and was hoping for a cure.

When the move to Connecticut finally arrived, Rob delivered his final insult. He was fearful I might take some of his furnishings, so afraid to let me move out without watching. It seemed unimaginable and selfish. Not only had I supported Rob's family, but after ten years, he still didn't have the slightest comprehension of my personality. He could only relate to how he or other selfish people might act under the same circumstances. He owed me a lot, but I didn't want his possessions. A "thank you" and "I'm sorry" would have sufficed. I had picked up all family bills and taken on his children as my stepfamily without any thanks. His attitude was the finishing blow.

There was no way that I could coordinate the moving weekend with small children underfoot, so he finally acquiesced and agreed to drive the kids out to the Hamptons on the last weekend in June, where there were other women around to supervise. After moving my things from the city apartment and from my storage room to the new Connecticut condo on Saturday, I drove three hours to and from the Hamptons on Sunday to get Liz and Ken. Amazingly, it all got done.

It was late in the evening, and the children were sleeping when we arrived at our new family home. As I climbed the stairs with Ken over my shoulder and Liz holding my hand, "Daisy Girl," an unexpected pet cat, made a surprise appearance to their sleepy but delighted amazement. I had told the previous owners they could leave her behind, as they were moving far away and had planned to put her to sleep. A peaceful night followed. The storm had quieted down.

The kids were prepared about what to expect, and the transition seemed to go smoothly. Divorce was never mentioned. I just said we were moving to a bigger place where they would have their own room and a swimming pool. Daddy would come to visit on the weekends. They didn't realize that the family was officially split until several years later.

Chapter 23

A Commuter Life

Excitement filled the morning air. The night before, the children each had their own room for the first time. The cat's meow was a morning hello, and the camp bus was waiting. Liz led the way, and Ken followed. They arrived home in the late afternoon shouting, "Yeah, camp!"

Greenwich was a breath of fresh air! I had stumbled on an oasis. Nature was in all its glory, with summer flowers in bloom. Our backyard bordered a conservation area displaying a hill filled with wildflowers. It led up to a charming, stone castle museum. I was eager to explore the inviting new ambiance. Quickly and unexpectedly, I fell in love with my new life. Although I had agonized over the idea of moving from Manhattan and splitting up the family, the move to Greenwich and the divorce proved to be the right choices.

Greenwich became the only place where my psyche ever felt truly comfortable. I finally had my own space and felt financially stable. My father's death also left me with some furniture, including my favorite bedroom set. After my father's house was sold, I could even put some money away for the children's college education. Our new condo would build equity—while eliminating the Manhattan private school and city living expenses. The air and outdoor play areas were far healthier for the children than the Manhattan community park sandbox where dogs urinated.

Soon after the move, I awoke with a start from a dream. Wade was plainly repeating several times, "Don't worry about me. I am all right." I hadn't thought about Wade since our spring meeting, so I tried to dismiss it as just a dream, but his voice wouldn't be ignored. When I called Sandra, she told me that Wade had died a few days before. Sandra and I both found comfort in his words and message. It was a clear voice that still remains vivid in my mind. It seemed to lie outside the apparent sensory boundaries within which we operate during our waking hours.

As I settled into Greenwich, the town and people came alive to me. After a car ride to the station, it was a comfortable 45-minute trip on Metro-North train to Manhattan, During the daily train ride, seated commuters generally had their heads in newspapers and books or stared out the windows. I usually chattered with Stephanie, a friend I met at a Newcomers' wine and cheese party. When we discovered we rode the same train, we arranged a meeting spot on the platform to ensure a fun commute.

Laughter accompanied stories about family and office during our train rides. Friendship bonds made our problems lighter. Stephanie had been a widowed single mother with two children living in Canada for many years before meeting her husband Bob on an airplane. She had a lot of empathy for my situation as a single, working mom. Newly married and employed as head of public relations for an international arts organization, she was starting a new life in Greenwich. Stephanie's two daughters were a few years older than my children, and she graciously invited my family to share Christmas dinner at her home. It continued for many years.

If I had understood the dramatic differences between the boring suburbia of my youth, and Greenwich, I would not have run so zealously from all suburbs. Greenwich is an active year-round community with ample parks, tennis, golf, restaurants, movie theaters and entertainment. Old money is the pillar of the town, but my baby boomer generation was moving in with their young families and it was changing.

Our condo community comprised seventy-seven Victorian-style townhouses built on tastefully-landscaped, rolling hills. There were bountiful azalea, rhododendrons and flowering trees from spring through summer. The resident' swimming pool and tennis court provided many hours of fun lounging by the pool with the kids and tennis parties for me.

A charming castle at the top of our hill was occupied by the Museum of Cartoon Art. History relates that the hill and valley had originally belonged to an ironworks factory. The owner built an all-cement castle for his mother, who was afraid of fires. The castle later became the museum, and the surrounding land was sold for private homes and our condos. My children would climb up to the castle, and a family season's pass for the museum allowed frequent admission. Sleigh riding was the hill's winter attraction.

Child support quickly stopped because Rob said, "I don't have the money." He was still encouraged to visit once a week by my feeding him dinner on Sunday nights and driving him to the train afterward. Since this was his second family, he could have walked away. I felt that the children should know their biological father, with all his strengths and weaknesses. They actually enjoyed more quality time from him on his weekend visits, even if it was mostly watching football games.

Now, over forty, I knew who I was and wasn't intimidated anymore. If I could handle Rob for ten years, I could manage anyone. I enjoyed being free to pick and choose friends for myself without having to answer to a dominating husband. Marriage to Rob had been emotionally draining, so I wanted to connect with kinder, more thoughtful types of people. I became more conscious of those who traveled to my music, and it led to a community of friends.

It often seems that destiny brought me to Round Hill Community Church. We stumbled on it at a Christmas fair during our first year. There was something special about it. The sign in the parlor announced, "The important thing about the various religions is not what distinguishes them from each other but what they have in common." This Community Church, nestled in back-country Greenwich, was independent of any outside organizations. The combination of interesting people with vibrant discussions, a brilliant minister, and an engaging Sunday school for the children made it the perfect connector.

Numerous compassionate people participated in the town government and community charities. I was drawn toward the dynamic members with kind hearts. Although I had drifted away from organized religion and returned mainly for the children, this wonderful community of stimulating fellowship sustained me for many years.

During our family's first official visit the following Thanksgiving, many preparations were underway for their annual Christmas pageant, and the casting call was out. Liz and Ken were intrigued by the attractive costumes and rushed to join in. An artistic parishioner found beautiful fabric and clothing in thrift shops, which she turned into stunning attire for the Sunday School's yearly play. I met Pat there, and we immediately clicked. Her effervescent and warm personality was inviting. Our children were similar ages, so our friendship developed, and she quickly included me as part of her extended family.

Ralph Ahlberg had just started as a new minister. His brilliant thinking and articulate expression brought a theological illumination about many subjects in the modern world. The principles of Christianity were inspirational in life, and members were free to openly discuss different perspectives on the particulars. Growth is a lifelong journey. The spirit must be nourished, or it is choked. An hour in the church was an hour of reflection furnishing renewed strength for the following week.

Vi, our Jamaican nanny, moved with us to Greenwich, but she no longer fit the children's needs. They needed someone who could read stories, play active games and drive to school activities. Vi was turning sixty-five and couldn't drive a car, so we agreed it was time for her to retire and live with the daughter, where she spent weekends. I paid her

Medicare Advantage plan for the next few years until she died of cancer. I was fortunate to have a mature woman for the six years.

Dougal, Ken's godfather, and his wife, Becky, were close friends while we lived in Manhattan, and it continued when they moved to the neighboring town of Darien. Our connection ran deep. They were our extended family for holiday dinners, special events and more. Katrina and Robbie, their two slightly-younger children, played well with Liz and Ken.

Lisa was the first and best of my younger American nanny experiences. Although she had left Iowa as a twenty-year-old seeking adventure and was the somewhat rebellious daughter of a schoolteacher, Lisa had common sense and solid values. Moreover, she enjoyed playing active games or reading stories, so was just what we needed. The kids loved her.

Ken was about six, and Liz was nine when we took our first family vacation with Lisa for a learn-to-ski week at Killington, Vermont. I had happy recollections of skiing in Aspen and Vermont before marriage but hadn't been on skis since I met Rob. While an avid water skier, snow skiing wasn't his sport, and Rob complained his back hurt on long car rides. Free again, I enthusiastically booked a week at a charming ski lodge and headed for Killington Mountain with the two children and our nanny in tow.

Skiing with a family is a dramatically different experience from doing it with friends. After the complex project of getting everyone geared for a day on the slopes and signing up for the week's ski lessons, Ken and Lisa both came down with the stomach flu and severe diarrhea. Ken rejoined his ski class a day and a half later. I was concerned that it was too early for him to return to skiing since restrooms were only at the base lodge. After the lifts closed at the end of the day, it was announced that Ken's class would be over an hour late. They were stuck up on the mountain. Waiting anxiously below, I imagined the worst.

They finally arrived. Apparently, the instructor was new to the mountain and accidentally took the beginner class down an expert slope. The young "hot dog" instructor chose the expert Black Diamond trail without checking trail maps. Ken was the only child who kept his skis on all the way down. With an adult helping, he had doggedly snowplowed between all the moguls to the base. After all my worry, Ken had a wonderful time and was awarded the expert Black Diamond pin as his trophy.

The next day it rained. Then it froze, and the "snow cat" machines chopped the frozen snow into "death pebbles." We persevered for the week, but the weather didn't cooperate.

After two years, Lisa decided to finish school and took an office job in New York City. Trusting a caregiver with your children's foundation years is an important decision and the next four nannies were failures. Of course, their agency employment applications never highlighted the many potential difficulties.

Dawn followed Lisa. Dawn, a sweet girl of nineteen, was trying to get away from a bad family situation. She had an alcoholic mother, a step-father who was having an affair with her under-age girlfriend, and a difficult younger sister with temper tantrums. She never knew her real father, but her second step-father lasted until she was fifteen. Dawn thought of him as her father because he was there for most of her youth. However, after her parents split up, she visited him with her seventeen-year-old girlfriend, and he began an affair with her friend, who teased Dawn about becoming her stepmother.

Dawn traveled across the country from Washington State to get away from her family and search for a secure, stable home environment. Unfortunately, I commuted to Manhattan every day and couldn't be her replacement parent. In the evenings, I could see her eyes were red from crying. After six months, she returned to Washington because her mother begged for help with her unruly younger sister. She did her nanny job well but hadn't established new emotional ties and felt obligated to her mother.

Since both children were now in school, the nanny criteria only required someone to work from 3 to 7 p.m. and on occasional weekends. It seemed like an easy job. However, local girls were even more of a problem than agency hires.

An advertisement in the local paper produced two short-term caretakers. The first one was okay but left after a month for an office job. Jen, the second, was a pretty girl who was more concerned with her social life than a job.

Fortunately, my brother's daughter came for a visit that summer. Joanne was graduating from high school and had won a scholarship to The Columbus School of Art. My brother asked if she could work for free at my office in Manhattan during the summer to gain experience on her resume. I hadn't seen Joanne for over ten years and worried that she might bring more problems. I hesitated and didn't have specific job for her at the office. As luck would have it, my receptionist suddenly announced she would be leaving that spring. Joanne became an excellent summer replacement.

My fears of her being difficult to manage like my brother were dispelled. Joanne was easy-going and cooperative. I became close to my niece and later to her sister Deborah. Deborah left home at the end of High School due to clashes with her father. I understood her pain. By the time Joanne appeared, my brother wasn't as strict, so that relationship was smoother. Both nieces returned in later years for visits, and we kept in touch by phone.

Joanne and Jen were close in age and seemed very compatible. They went out to socialize on the Friday evening when Jo arrived. Sunday, I just happened to go to Jen's bedroom and was surprised to find it cleaned out. A note was left saying, "I will not be back." Jen had calculated that Joanne would take her place. Thankfully, Joanne pitched right in and worked as the nanny until I could hire one through a service. Then Joanne finished out the summer working in my office.

Holly, a very overweight farm girl and vegetarian, wrote assuredly on her application that she had no problem cooking meat or any meal that I might instruct for the family. However, under her care, the kids learned to cook in the microwave for themselves, and I had to buy fifteen boxes of cereal each week to keep her fed. After her initial honeymoon on the job, she became sloppy, leaving mounds of clothes around. She also seemed to spend an inordinate amount of time on the phone.

When the phone bill arrived a couple of months late, it was huge and included charges for her calls the previous two months—many of which were long-distance calls to Brazil. Confronted, she admitted hiding the first bills that arrived and then announced she was quitting. In addition to leaving me with the invoices, she backed my car into a red sports car in the Pizza Hut parking lot during the last week. Dawn had also backed into a car, so the two accidents together caused me the Connecticut high-risk insurance group rates for the next seven years.

After four nannies in one year, I was quite exasperated. In Europe, being a nanny to improve English skills was a desirable profession, so I went to the Au Pair USA service. While au pairs were limited to thirteen months in the country, my hopes of getting someone who stayed longer had faded.

Katja from Germany was our first European au pair. She was kind but firm, which was just what Ken needed. He was at a challenging age and a nuisance, made worse by Holly's carelessness on schoolwork and any type of structure. One time I came home to find Kenny tied to the stair banister. I knew she was doing it in jest and to teach a lesson, so I just laughed. He was an awful irritant, and Katja was a kind person, so it was quite funny. She would like to have stayed beyond the thirteen-month limit, and I would have kept her.

Next was a French au pair. Christelle was petite, only 5'2", but several brothers had taught her how to handle boys surprisingly well. She was also pretty and hip, which got Kenny's attention. My hope was that her French might help Liz learn her school language, but Christelle came to learn English, so that is what was spoken. Again, I would have kept her longer, and she would have stayed, but she had to leave when the time was up.

After Christelle left, Liz and Ken were too old for a nanny, but I still needed someone to enforce homework and drive to activities. I went back to the newspaper and hired pathetic Ann Marie. She appeared fine at the interview but later proved to be very dysfunctional and undisciplined. Her mother had kicked her out of the house and wouldn't take her back.

Somehow she put a hundred miles a day on my car, "just driving around." It was an accident waiting to happen. Repeated requests to drive a maximum of thirty miles a day were ignored entirely. One evening, I came home to find the kids had been left alone all afternoon. She was fired that night. That was the last straw. I moved my office into the basement.

As many single, working moms know, it is difficult to replace a wife or supportive husband. Even with a capable nanny, there are generally no delicious dinners waiting on the table or someone to share the day at work. While they provide laughs about the day's events with the children, there is a gap. The younger nannies are similar to an older daughter, and some may create difficulties. Older professional nannies with business references may avoid some problems, but they are more expensive and may play less with the children. There is an inevitable turnover in all cases, which leaves a new learning curve for both sides.

As I look back, they were short, precious years.

Chapter 24

The Precious Years

Children are diamonds in the rough. The grade school years are a fleeting, precious time of their unconditional love—a time to enjoy and polish their skills and values while you are the light of their life. It won't last. Their achievements and the glittering art creations they bring home from school should be proud moments or moments when we are alerted to get more involved.

One of the advantages of moving to Greenwich was their top-rated learning disability program. Liz's first grade class in Greenwich included Mr. P., a supportive tutor who gave her self-confidence and motivation along with class lessons. She was capable of learning, but easily distracted in classrooms, so she needed individual attention.

Before the testing and discovery of her difficulty, Liz had trouble writing letters. I broke each letter into the components of straight lines, slant lines, circles and half-circles, and it worked. While school could be a struggle, she learned that perseverance paid off and asked for help when needed.

During a parent-teacher discussion, her teacher paled when I mentioned that "she could always hire an accountant." In the back of my mind was Pam, from our beach house and wedding. Pam had learning difficulties, but her determination to succeed proved her teachers wrong, and she became a huge success. She gave me hope that Liz could succeed in spite of her learning disadvantage. I knew Liz had her father's sales strengths, which the school's math department did not appreciate. However, Liz's school problems added to the complexity of being a working mother.

Ken was the opposite, with strong logical-sequential abilities. He displayed my father's analytic method of thinking and had exceptional gifts for both math and writing. Teachers loved his long, interesting stories when other children were just writing a few sentences. A couple of his short stories, "The Scales of the Sewer Snake" and "The Executor," were published in the classroom; they still sit on our bookshelves.

Taking it for granted that Ken would always be a good student, I sometimes let him con me into believing he completed his homework. It allowed me to put more of my available time into Liz's assignments and study with her for exams. It is easier to correct bad habits before they become too ingrained.

Condos are often filled with retired people or childless couples—but not our townhouses. The rolling hills with second floors, basements and outside steps made older residents move out, and the baby boomers move in with their families. Three-bedroom units with open play areas attracted parents with young children. Mothers could socialize at the community pool and tennis court while entertaining their kids. Ken and his friends loved to race up and down the steps with their skateboards until the Board of Directors put an end to the activity. It was a fun place for kids to grow up. Children had playmates without a car trip, and the parents met friends.

Town activities included Cub Scouts and Brownies. Families cheered as they watched scout troops march down the avenue in parades and often joined overnight scout camping expeditions—sleeping in tents at a local reservation.

"Having it all" included having pets. All of our neighbors knew and loved "Frisko," our Siamese cat. On my forty-seventh birthday, I received a tearful call at the office from the children tragically relating that he had been killed by a car that afternoon. Instead of a birthday party, we had a sad and tearful funeral. The neighborhood children were dressed in black to deliver their eulogies at a burial on our hillside. The following birthday, I had Chicken Pox, passed down from Ken to Liz and myself. My gift was not getting permanent scars.

It was too demanding to monitor the doors to keep a cat inside, so after two cats were killed by cars on our private streets, we stayed with caged rabbits, fish, a lizard, hamsters, a frog and gerbils. None could compare to "Izzy," the gerbil who would obey my command and liked to cuddle.

Izzy had a personality and became known by the neighborhood. She was trained to run into my hands from anywhere in the room when called by name. It started when I let Izzy run around the table while cleaning the cage. If she returned to my open hands, she received a petting and fresh food. Izzy first jumped off the table accidentally but returned when called. She would sometimes run around the room for a half-hour, and spectators were amazed that she would return from anywhere. One time she accidentally got stuck behind the kitchen stove. Since Fire Departments were reputed to help cats in trees, I called them. An entire unit responded to save one little gerbil. The incident provided chuckles around town for weeks.

I did my best to get home from work by 7 p.m. A busy evening was ahead. After running the business, I regularly checked homework and helped Liz understand assignments. I questioned why they had put her on a different math track when she entered high school. A well-meaning Special Ed Department teacher gave her opinion that Liz "not college material" in our parent meeting. Determined to provide every possible opportunity, I convinced the department to change their objectives. Then I read the geometry textbook with Liz, reviewed assignments and spent many nights and weekends coaching for tests. An outside tutor was hired for algebra.

Traditional Holidays were gathering times of family and friends, a time to catch up with people who sometimes lived far away, by phone if not in person. Creating special family memories filled with fun, food and socializing evoked fond recollections and laughter.

Thanksgiving was usually at our home. Becky and Dougal's family, Rob and occasional other guests were invited. Everyone would contribute their favorite dishes to a mouthwatering turkey feast.

Easter Sundays were spent at Dougal's lovely home on the water in Darien. After a delicious lamb meal, everyone took a walk to hunt for Easter eggs. The night before, pre-Easter fun included drawing designs or names on hard-boiled eggs, with eggs symbolizing a new birth or beginning. Baskets with treats would await the children in the morning, and each person got an egg inscribed with their name at the Sunday meal.

Christmas became a yearly event with my train buddy, Stephanie, her daughters and her husband, Bob. Her sister's family and two nieces were usually present when we all celebrated with the Canadian tradition of "Christmas Crackers." Stephanie placed a colorful, segmented cardboard tube with a prize in the central chamber at each place setting before dinner. The Christmas Cracker would get pulled apart by two people, each holding an outer handle. A snapping sound and the laughter of friends heralded the winners, who held the main chamber and prize.

I watched her two beautiful daughters grow from teens to married doctors and lawyers. Stephanie would graciously loan her husband, Bob, to help install shelves or heavyweight tasks when needed. When we first met, Bob was looking for a career after early military retirement, and he subsequently became a teacher for learning-disabled students. He was an attractive man with a very kind heart. Knowing my friend's husbands renewed my belief in compassionate men.

Halloween was the time to carve pumpkins. Before cutting, we washed away the messy insides to extract the pumpkin seeds, then spread them out on a tray to salt and bake for a snack. Of course, the Halloween highlight was dressing up in costumes to "trick or treat" the neighborhood. Our condo was a very safe community—with many neighbors and children participating in the fun. One man was always a hit. He answered the doorbell dressed up as Darth Vader and played the part.

As preteens, they went to a charming sleepover camp at the picturesque Lake Winnipesaukee in New Hampshire, while my childcare was on vacation. I took vacation time simultaneously with enjoyable side trips. I maximized the vacation as a relaxing, scenic drive to visit surrounding areas.

Liz and Ken's first overnight camp was located in New Hampshire near an exquisite lakeside setting. Camp Brookwoods, a non-denominational Christian camp, included sports, pillow fights, campfires, games, swimming and more. Since young minds soak up ideas and I was often an absentee parent, I hoped the healthy spiritual life and ethical values promoted by the camp would fill in some gaps and build inner strength to face the world's challenges.

At age fourteen Liz became ineligible the sleep-away camp, so she scheduled a biking adventure group departing from Boston. After Ken was settled at camp on Lake Winnipesaukee, Liz and I travelled for several days before heading to Boston, visiting friends near Lake Sunapee, spending a night in charming Portsmouth, N. H. and driving a little way into Maine. In Boston, Laura and Allie joined us for a reunion meal. When we arrived at the airport to meet the group, there was no bus! It was the wrong day. The good news was we were a day early for the biking trip and not late.

My busy life hadn't allowed much vacation time since Liz was born. However, I had begun to date again. One man gave sagacious advice. He wisely said, "Memories are built from special family times, and children will remember vacations. No one will ever put on your tombstone that you are a hard worker." If he hadn't urged me to take some longer trips, I might have missed the wonderful times entirely.

The first family airplane adventure was to Disney World in 1993. Ken was 11 and Liz 14, suitable ages to enjoy a full range of activities with me, including foreign foods, shows and educational exhibits. We only had a few hours on the evening of our arrival, so we headed to "Pleasure Island," a largely over-21 party and drinking area. It was also pleasantly filled with entertaining surprises for children, such as talking masks telling stories.

At the advice of my friend, Pat, we were up at 7 a.m. to be early on the lines at the park. Being early enabled us to miss many of the long lines on popular rides and shows. Numerous rides, photo-ops with oversized Disney characters, parades, fireworks and superb stage shows were a never-ending supply of entertainment.

The more educational area was Epcot Center—where each country had a building with a ride through narrated exhibits; they frequently offered tasty foods from their country to sample. Everywhere had family fun and enjoyable entertainment in well-planned theme parks. The Magic Kingdom, Epcot Center, MGM Studios and Universal Studios offered marvelous days of fabulous fun for the week.

Our destination spot for spring break 1995 was Washington D.C. Liz and Ken were both learning about our country's history in school, so the timing was appropriate. We encountered sunny weather during cherry blossom season, and walked all over the city. Attractions included the fascinating Smithsonian museums, a tour of the president's White House residence, the Mint, a show at Ford's Theater, and the

Spy Museum. Our vacation ended with a Kennedy Center performance of the hilarious whodunit, *Sheer Madness.* This family vacation supplied a valuable introductory understanding of our government and the U.S.'s part in world influence.

Liz, still a light sleeper, heard a mugging outside our hotel window during the night, so she was uneasy about Washington until many years later, when she would love living and working there.

The following summer, Liz enjoyed being a counselor at a YWCA camp. She loved to play with kids but had a powerful, commanding voice when needed, so she was excellent at the job.

Coincidentally, I met a lifetime friend from the camp connection. There weren't any interesting men to meet at a singles party in the Bruce Museum, so a spark of attraction made me walk up to Elizabeth. We discovered Liz was her daughter's counselor. Both of us were single business moms with a lot in common. Liz became her babysitter when their nanny was away. Elizabeth and I bonded.

Chapter 25

The Ties That Bind

I often had an uncanny sense for matching people to business positions. Now I put it to use in my personal life. After forty, a clearer identity emerged. Finding lasting relationships works best when you know yourself.

It was wonderful to be free from a dominating husband's constraints and have life experiences to draw on. Rob had dictated our relationships with other couples by how he felt about the man. The man had to be fun and laugh at his jokes, or he would object to my inviting the couple to dinner. Now when I was interested in making friends with a couple, I acted on it. I consciously looked for connections among likely groups and followed where they led. Those who were self-confident and friendly often radiated the right sparks—showing the way on my treasure hunt.

I was single in a couple's world. Some well-meaning Manhattan friends had warned that I would be ostracized in a married suburban community, but I wasn't shunned. "After forty" presented a unique time in life when socialization isn't all about dating. It was enjoyable talking with accomplished, secure women and learning from those with successful marriages. Their warm, understanding ways became priceless. Friends blended, and created a stable extended family atmosphere.

After the first year in Connecticut organizing my family and home, I joined the Newcomers' Club.

The Greenwich Newcomers' Club, run by the YWCA, organized a wine and cheese party at someone's home the second Friday of every month. They were lively parties in lovely large homes that could accommodate the crowd. Everyone brought an appetizer for four and paid a token amount toward the wine provided by the hostess. Since all were married couples, I pretended that I had a husband in the next room and wandered about chatting with various people who caught my eye. To nurture relationships, however, there has to be planned follow-up.

If you offer to cook, friends don't care if you're single or with a date. Most people are open to an invitation to play. I invited two or three couples over for dinner or tennis parties. Matching compatible people was more important than having a single or two in the group. There were always two or three men, so they could have "man talk" when they wanted. I picked enjoyable people and was determined to enjoy my life in suburbia without a man. It was a tremendous feeling of liberation.

In addition to the monthly parties, I participated in a sub-group from the club formed to support the purchase of season tickets for the Greenwich Symphony Orchestra. The orchestra performed five times a year in the high school auditorium.

Our amicable group of friends always had animated stories to tell, so a simple potluck dinner party before the concert at someone's home provided a fun social evening. An evening in Manhattan often involved a pricey performance ticket and restaurant dinner plus an hour of travel. Having local town entertainment was a worthwhile activity to support and promote. Eventually, the original group became too large for one home, so some couples split off. As the only single, I was left with a few newer couples.

I seized the opportunity to create a select group of friends to form my own group, adding other couples that I knew from church to a total of around twenty. Included were Stephanie and Bob, Pat and Ray, plus a new couple—Jane and John, and Caroline and Win—professor friends from church. Every year I lined up five houses for the five concerts and printed a schedule dividing the food assignments into two entrees, two appetizers, two desserts, and salad and bread. The hostess would make changes if needed and supply the wine.

The chemistry between everyone was a great success. Many wonderful, long-lasting friendships resulted. It's been a winner since 1988, spreading, growing and adapting to life changes for over fifteen years. Life's full of tough stuff, and we all need a tribe when we are down and out. Our group was that tribe, always there for each other when needed.

I've been very fortunate to have companions to invite for dinner, men in my life, extended family for the holidays, and an enduring group of enjoyable friends. We enjoyed outings to many places. A favorite occasion was the "Chihuly Exhibit" at the Brooklyn Botanical Garden, followed by a delicious Italian dinner on Arthur Avenue, well known for its authentic Italian cuisine. My life would have been very different without those friends. If things got rough, they were my support system.

When Stephanie's family grew large with marriages and grandchildren, Pat and Ray became my extended family for Christmas. Over the years, Pat was always there for times of crisis and fun. When Liz was trying to lose weight as a young teenager, she introduced us to hypnosis. Pat managed a hypnosis clinic, dealing with smoking, focus, weight loss, and other issues. Since Pat is a definite "type A" high energy personality, it was hard to imagine her soothing others in a hypnotic voice. However, I've seen her do it—at my dinner table. A friend expressed his disbelief at a dinner party. Within two minutes, he was in a trance.

Pat's husband Ray taught an excellent practical math course for high school students. I wish had been around when I went to school. This class in personal finance reviewed the *Wall Street Journal* daily and discussed how it would affect their lives. He also discussed credit cards, student loans, gave them a theoretical salary to live on, and much more.

Essential to successful friendships with couples are trust and compatibility. I never flirted, encouraged or acted on any sparks with a married man. It was the friendship that I valued most. A stable girlfriend can last well into old age. Relationships with men are more complex and married men were not of interest.

Most of my friendships were exceptionally satisfying and long-lasting. A couple didn't fall into that category, but I enjoyed the rapport while it lasted. A neighbor friend turned out to be damaged by an unfaithful husband and became very jealous. It often takes unwavering determination or therapy to undo emotional baggage that makes relationships difficult or impossible.

Just before the July 4th fireworks, Ken met Bret at our condo's pool, and the boys hit it off as playmates. We met up again at the high school July 4th fireworks display. His mother lived in our condo community, so his father, Charlie, and I enjoyed each other's company when our sons had play dates. Later Charlie became Ken's Cub Scout leader. Ironically, Charlie's company was similar to Rob's business, but had a factory and was more extensive. We had many similar interests, including the graphic arts and computers, but not romantic sparks.

I introduced Charlie to my neighborhood friend, Sue, a pretty, twice-divorced woman and mother of four. They started dating. One night, Charlie and I decided to order pizza for dinner when he was over picking up Bret from a play date. Sue called, so I invited her to join us, but she declined. The next day she was enraged because I had dared to have dinner with her boyfriend. She had lost her last ex-husband to his secretary, so she lived with jealousy and distrust of all other women.

Her past messed up her future and made her quick to assume guilt without proof. Neither Charlie nor I could deal with her paranoia, so she lost both my close friendship and her boyfriend. Moreover, if the chemistry had been right, I was there first. This accusation was unwarranted.

Distrust and jealousy blind people to the facts. A few months later, Charlie started dating a chatty woman who was very independent and trusting. I remained a friendly neighbor to Sue, but we no longer socialized.

After our move to Connecticut, Rob seemed to get by, and I didn't ask questions. One day he surprised me by announcing, "The bank is foreclosing on the Hampton beach house, and I will lose everything." He had been digging himself deeper into debt by mortgaging the house.

I couldn't let the bank take it, knowing beach real estate in the Hamptons would sell quickly. I bailed him out. Rob's track record showed he couldn't be trusted with the money, so a lawyer wrote up a three-month bridge mortgage, stipulating that I would directly pay the bank's invoices. Rob fulfilled his promise to sell the property; I received interest on my loan, and he could pay off his debts for a fresh start with a small amount of cash remaining.

I tried to shield Ken and Liz from their father's money problems. The daughters claimed anything they wanted from the beach house, and I received a few items. The rest was given away. It was a sad ending for a lot of memories.

A few months later, a mutual friend inquired whether I knew of a rental room for someone who needed a weekday location in Manhattan. I suggested Rob's spare bedroom, as he needed money. Sophia was a paralegal headhunter in Manhattan and participated in the Hampton group houses, so we knew many of the same people. She owned a charming house about an hour north of me in Connecticut and sometimes stayed overnight at my condo to socialize on the way back to her home on weekends. We would attend a single's party in my area or just go out to dinner. Commiserating about living with Rob, being single, or the latest man in our life produced a lot of laughter. A great friendship developed, sharing fun times and career interests.

I told Rob's middle daughter, Jennifer, that she was welcome to bring her girlfriend to my new home, but she was not satisfied. She had recently moved back to the East Coast and "come out of the closet." I didn't see it coming.

Of course, she was entitled to her personal choice, but it was not a way of life that I wanted for my family. I wanted grandchildren and my traditional values. She wanted something I was unable to give— full approval of her lesbian lifestyle and to be very close to my daughter. I'm ever mindful that simple comments and actions reverberate for years. Separate philosophic principles are able to coexist in a friendly way, so I couldn't understand her all or nothing attitude.

I did a lot for their family but selfishly hoped for old age as a grandmother. I just couldn't go that extra mile of embracing her decision. We have to be our authentic selves. Parents have a right and duty to instill their perceived ideals in their children. She opened a Pandora's box, which I didn't know how to handle.

Perhaps she wanted unconditional love, and I was unable to give it. Jennifer's easy-to-ignite anger was incensed, and after that, she just tolerated me in her father's presence. Neither of us could become a different person, but I was supposed to violate my values and was not allowed my gut feelings, something I couldn't deny in myself.

Her father was also unhappy with her choice but didn't want to make any more problems. He recognized himself as probably part of the reason for her anger against men.

Families will affect us in many ways. Connecting with our family's historical values and heritage fills an innate need in each one of us to connect with our past and learn from mistakes. The way we relate to our roots adds to a strong sense of who we really are and establishes a unique core identity.

"To every bird, his nest is beautiful."

—Italian Proverb

Chapter 26

The Resourceful Chameleon

Adaptability is vital to survival; it minimizes risk. In the animal kingdom, many creatures transform themselves in order to persist. Chameleons are considered the "quick-change artists" but are not very fast-moving. Other creatures are much more agile. Cuttlefish receive color-changing instructions directly from their brains, helping them to both grab a quick meal and avoid becoming one for others. The mimic octopus not only revamps its pattern on a dime but changes the very shape of its body to imitate a sea snake, a lionfish, or a piece of floating coral. Salamanders can regenerate limbs and eyes as needed.

Some quick changes were needed to get through a battlefield of ongoing challenges. I wrote a letter responding to the retroactive tax invoice addressed to my closed corporation, and the government never pursued collection. Our unemployment case was not well- publicized, so competition flourished for a while under the old system, without our added costs. However, we adapted to the transformation by cutting costs and splitting the company into two new corporations; half of the company became a temporary employment agency, and the other half represented independent contractors. The market eventually became an equal playing field again. After making changes needed for the unemployment case, a new hurdle appeared on the horizon.

Recessions almost always come as a surprise— even though they seem easy to explain after the fact. The recession of 1990-91 peaked in 1990 but began before. Debt accumulations, a jump in oil prices after Iraq invaded Kuwait, manufacturing being moved offshore as the provisions of NAFTA kicked in, a credit crunch induced by overzealous banking regulators, and the attempt by the Federal Reserve to lower the rate of inflation have all been cited as causes. In 1989 the New York real estate market was going through turmoil and collapsing. Companies were going out of business, and rents were dropping.

One unhappy Monday in 1989, I found our architect tenants had moved out over the weekend. Although a successful relationship for eight years, they closed their company suddenly, running out on their lease by leaving a year early without warning, and sticking my company with additional payments. Our rent skyrocketed.

If you enjoy taking risks, financial perils are an entrepreneur's survive-or-die game. Finding a similar tenant for the same rent in a slow market was impossible. I tried to negotiate with the building agents, but they attempted to manipulate a woman and not compromise. They wouldn't agree to any deal or take back the unused space, even though we had been dependable tenants for nine years.

Running out on a lease was not something I considered ethical or wanted to do. Staying, however, would be business and financial suicide. I had watched Rob lose everything and wasn't going to repeat that mistake. One of life's many moral dilemmas is at what point to draw the line and save your hide. Sooner or later, the lease would be broken.

A real estate broker friend advised, "Simply move out! Since the original dissolved corporation had signed the lease and the agents have been accepting checks from a different corporate name, it will be very complicated for a landlord to collect anything." We simply relocated across the street at 25 West 45th Street. Our friendly building superintendent helped us move out on the weekend and was very understanding. Both the original corporation and office were now closed, but the business continued.

I happened upon the building owner when I was back at the old office collecting items. He couldn't believe that the renting agent wouldn't strike a deal. Realizing that I had been a dependable tenant for nine years, he said he would have compromised but wasn't told of the dilemma. There was no effort to collect.

The new offices were very pleasant, and the business cruised from a new port. Our staffing business took a financial hit from the legal verdict, so capital and income were lower; we survived by cutting staff and office size. Bernie's methods did pay off, and the illustration division became profitable. There were sunny days for a while, but neither of us could foresee the next tidal wave. Another reinvention was about to happen.

Just as the illustration division grew to a respectable size, computer advancements changed the art market. First, stock art became available on the internet and often replaced original illustration. Hungry artists sold the rights to their work to gain fast money, and cheap art flooded the market. New software innovations enabled designers to interpret from stock art without hiring an illustrator. In addition, the art schools kept graduating new talent willing to work for any price. The resulting illustration industry shrank to only a fraction of its original size.

Simultaneously, technology increased productivity and profits by eliminating employees. Computers were replacing departments of people in many businesses. A few computer artists could handle the work of many traditional designers and production personnel, so large art departments were minimized.

Administrative temp agencies began to test Photoshop and other design software, so our temp agency competition also increased. At first, their placement counselors had no ability to critique talent other than a test score, but eventually they hired skilled people and competed voraciously for our business.

Some large temp agencies successfully negotiated economically favorable deals with human resource departments for an exclusive on creative along with their usual administrative temps. Our regular clients were forced to use a designated large agency.

Technology transformations and cost-cutting modifications required many companies to undergo staff restructuring. A prominent New York public utility company had been a steady client for years, but an efficiency expert converted our long-term freelancers to staff.

Political muscle even eased us out of WBE (Women's Business Enterprise) contracts—that were supposed to encourage women in business. The WBE certification, consisting of reams of paperwork, was required to get The Long Island Railroad, NYTA and MTA contracts. While they were satisfied customers for many years, suddenly large agencies pushed us out with their commanding sales connections and showmanship at a higher level. They held the higher, powerful cards. Money can manipulate circumstances.

Technology kept growing at an unprecedented rate. Earlier in the cycle, I might have used my temp business to leverage a deal with a larger company, but was now outmaneuvered. Although I was adapting quickly, the expansion happened faster than I thought possible, and the full consequences of the computer in my business were not foreseen.

Fortunately, I saw what was happening before it hit rock bottom. I could see a cliff on the horizon and prepare for the worst. All our major contracts were expiring within a year, so I decided to take as much profit as possible, and then move my office to my home in Connecticut at lease-end. Staff had to be cut, offices were sublet, and I started doing everyone's job. Laying-off loyal people was difficult, but I had to survive.

The first to go was Gina, my two-day-a-week computer-billing operator. She had been infected with hepatitis from raw seafood and was frequently out sick, so she was the natural first choice.

Bernie was the highest paid, so he had to go. Bernie was as close as I came to a business partner but differed in that he pulled a decent steady salary while I took all the financial risk. Fortunately, he had obtained his Master's degree at night, so he set up in private practice as a therapist. I sadly let Elaine go after twelve years of loyal service. She had done her job well and had difficulty understanding how the industry picture changed for us all. In the end, I had the business and another challenge to reinvent revenue.

Tom Gong, an intelligent, handsome Chinese entrepreneur with a friendly smile and personality, rented an empty office. We had many informative conversations. I assisted him with business questions, and he showed me the internet when it went public in April 1993. It was incredible to see the web transport images and information for the first time. Telephone line internet connections were very slow, but amazing. He assured me the internet would be the way of the future.

The only full-time employee to remain was Sara, who lived near my home in Connecticut. At the end of the lease, I planned to close the current office and work from home with Sara. A home office would also allow some supervision of Liz and Ken. Ages twelve and fifteen were too old for babysitters and too young to be alone.

That last year in the city was very profitable because the overhead was so low. However, the writing was clearly on the wall.

As I began closing the office, I thought of the challenges and triumphs over the years. I was fortunate to have many enthusiastic employees believing in our cause. They put their heart into the business, helping people find employment while enjoying their creative talents.

Most office furniture had to be thrown out, abandoned or given away. Whatever could be salvaged from a seven-office suite was stuffed into my garage and basement.

For the first year, I maintained a single executive office near Grand Central Terminal to interview candidates, meet with clients and work with Hilde, my bookkeeper. A new internet company named "Yahoo" also rented a large office on the same floor for their startup. After a year, I totally closed the Manhattan presence, and Hilde, my bookkeeper for over twelve years, retired.

The pursuit of happiness always leads to the next quest. We have to accept this world and perfect the skill of reinventing. Making it an adventure is a state of mind and an urging of the human spirit.

It has sometimes been a roller-coaster, but being an entrepreneur has also been an exciting adventure and transforming experience. "Maybe something fabulous will happen next." I didn't see it then, but technology would open up a new exciting opportunity in my future on the internet.

Rob was getting old and steadily going downhill. His condition could have created a very negative image for the children, so I gave him a part-time job doing sales calls in my Manhattan office; I paid him an hourly rate for a couple of days a week. He finally learned more about my business. Still an excellent opener on the phone, he did manage to bring in some new clients, but it was too late; the market had dried up to the point of no return. I tried to teach him some basic computer skills, and he attempted to learn, but Rob was a dinosaur in a world that he couldn't understand.

One day he said, "I am officially going bankrupt." I was shocked. Rob declared that bankruptcy was the only way to clear the record for a failed investment of our college fund. Until then, I didn't know it had been sold. In our separation agreement, some land, worth about two years of tuition, was put aside for our children's college education. It had been sold without my knowledge and invested in a mini-warehouse partnership deal, another get-rich-quick scheme that failed.

With bankruptcy, his debtors couldn't come after him for a failed partnership. A few final payout checks had been received by him and quickly spent. The small profit he had made on the beach house sale was gone. The entire college burden was left to me, along with their yearly support since birth.

Chapter 27

Fun at Fifty

During a lifetime, many dreams are dashed like ocean waves and then reborn at sunrise to calm seas. Love finally arrived by my 50th birthday. On the birthday that many women dread, I was ecstatic. My fifties became fun years, not over-the-hill flavorless years. They were times filled with romance, reunions and rewarding new relationships.

For several years after the move to Greenwich, I was glad to be free again. A sense of relief flooded over me, and I was not looking for another man. Business and a young family created a full and busy life. Eventually, I wistfully thought that just maybe, it might be possible to find a self-sufficient, stable companion with high integrity who was generally agreeable. That must have been too idealistic, as the few single gatherings around the time were unproductive. In the days before internet dating, not many promising avenues were available. Luck had to enter the picture. Cupid entered my life at a Super Bowl party a few months before my 50th birthday.

Andy and I hit it off immediately, and romantic sparks were ignited. Within two months, it was love.

My new amour was a distinguished gentleman with white hair and a warm smile. Our song was "Unforgettable." His song to me was Roy Orbison's, "Anything you want, you got it!" He was genuinely compassionate. Unlike Rob, Andy actually cared and listened to what went on during my day as we chatted in excellent restaurants. There were absorbing conversations, fun dinners and shared interests. Andy was one of the rare men in my life who noticed and complimented my accomplishments or how I looked and dressed.

Andy, a partner in a well-established accounting firm, was seven years my senior with a comfortable home in Connecticut and a beach house on Nantucket Island. His only marriage of twenty years had produced two lovely grown daughters. I embraced having finally found Mr. Right.

As an added benefit, Andy was a gourmet cook. His cooking influenced my children to try it. Ten-year-old Kenny took up cooking and successfully made quite complicated recipes and delicious cheesecakes. It started after my return home from an emergency room visit for an infected toe. Liz and Ken had brunch waiting. Seizing upon the idea, I suggested they alternate weeks to prepare meals for their father's Sunday visit. I would purchase the ingredients and help with any recipe they picked. Liz chose the more everyday meals, but Ken looked for the most complicated recipe he could find and then followed the instructions meticulously.

The Andy affair was wonderful—until his dark side began to emerge. After about five months, we started having minor conflicts generated by weekend trips to Nantucket. His beach house was rented out most of the summer; he expected me to travel there every weekend in May, June and September–an over six-hour drive each way. Moreover, if the two children joined us, they were expected to sit quietly in the back seat for the long trip. Although Nantucket was a charming beach community, weekend trips were too stressful. I worked all week and didn't want to leave the children with the au pair on my time off. He was perturbed that I would only go occasionally.

His anger bubbled beneath the surface and exploded the following September. As we approached Nantucket and stopped at a supermarket, he flew into an uncontrollable verbal rage over nothing. It started at the store and lasted throughout the evening. A totally different person emerged. His arguments didn't make sense and were occasionally incoherent. His eyes darted back and forth. I stared at him in shock and fear. Andy looked and acted like a madman. My heart began pounding with the thought that he might be physically violent. I was alone with him in a house on an island, distant from any neighbors. I spoke calmly and assuredly to his wild accusations for several hours, doing what I could to diffuse his anger. He eventually fell asleep.

The following day he apologetically said that when he didn't have food in his system, the lack of sugar in his brain could make him very irritable. I forgave him but knew something was amiss.

Manic behavior is something people didn't generally discuss, and the ramifications were vague in my mind. Later, I learned his mother had been institutionalized at the end of her life. Obviously, a predisposition to a worrisome shade of the abnormality had appeared. He was never physically violent, but it sometimes seemed he would snap.

Small tantrums grew more frequent over trivial and petty things. The following day a gorgeous flower arrangement would always arrive with an apology. Two definite personalities surfaced. One was fun and relaxed, and the other was controlling and bizarre.

I tried to end the relationship numerous times, but he would arrive on my doorstep and beg for forgiveness with flowers. As his last chance, he talked me into meeting with a marriage counselor. The clever therapist had us each calmly describe our side of the situation. I explained my fear of his anger and listed various examples. Andy then listed his justifications for getting angry and my failures. The therapist concluded that if I had issues and Andy had explanations, he couldn't help us. He politely shook our hands and led us toward the door.

Andy knew this meant that the relationship was over. As we got near the door, his steps slowed down. Then he stopped, swallowed hard and changed his story saying, "It's not her fault." The therapist quickly signed him up to come back for individual anger-management sessions. I hoped for the improbable, and therapy helped, but years of habit and genetic predisposition cannot be broken entirely.

Finally, two years after the relationship started, he had one of his fits, and I refused to take him back. I used the transferring of office to home as an excuse, saying time was needed. By stalling for several weeks, the fire of the moment had subsided, and I finalized the break-up on the phone.

My divorce was a relief, but this break-up left a painful emptiness. There were many cherished times, and I missed the Andy who had been a very nurturing companion. Pat took me to the U.S. Open with the kids, trying to help me forget and forge new memories. She was always there to help, and her energy redirected my psyche for the day.

Relationships will fade with time unless you make an effort to keep them alive. I knew my relationship was intrinsically flawed. One morning several months later, I woke up, and Andy was part of history.

We all want "unconditional love"—a relationship that will stick forever through highs and lows. However, love can be destroyed. Successful relationships take work on both sides, and true love doesn't always get its own way. I don't believe there is unconditional love in romance, just some people who might put up with more abuse than others. True, lasting love should fill our lives with compassion, kindness and respect. It is not selfish or abusive.

Several months later, at a Red Cross Benefit in Greenwich, I was surprised to see Gene, a boyfriend from my twenties. We hit it off again and dated for several months. He had remained a bachelor, worked hard and then sold his business for a sizeable profit. While we enjoyed each other's company, it still wasn't the right match. Moreover, he was eleven years my senior and I didn't want another older man. I was young for my years, and life was getting short. He understood.

After a few months, I moved on again by trying a dating service. The service sent a guy that seemed appropriate at first but the agency wasn't faithful to my request for a man within five years of my age. Joe was fifteen years my senior—even older than Gene.

I looked elsewhere. Singles parties were getting more frequent, but I didn't want to run into Andy. I tried a pre-internet dating service; photos were placed in books, and video clips were available for viewing. Their list of questions was a revealing way of thinking about who would make an appropriate match, rather than just the luck of the draw at a party. I contacted someone who attracted my interest, and it became a two-year romance.

Lee was a handsome man with a terrific sense of humor and an entertaining imagination. His favorite sport was baseball—in particular, the Boston Red Sox. Baseball was not one of my interests, but I enjoyed any camaraderie that surrounded it. Pat and Ray thought it would be a great outing to see a Boston Red Sox game, so the four of us traveled to a game at Fenway Park, then delighted in touring around Boston's historic and shopping areas.

Pat and Ray were always ready for entertainment. They held wonderful black-tie New Year's Eve parties at their home. The men enjoyed getting some use out of their tuxedos, and the women felt glamorous in beautiful dresses. We pitched in for food and enjoyed Pat's gourmet dinner at a large, elegantly-decorated table. As I watch the scenes captured by my video camera, I smile with warm memories.

Owning a business filled any gambling need in me. Still I enjoyed a trip to the Foxwoods Casino when, one of Lee's nephews graduated from college. Lee's brother provided complimentary bonus tickets covering everything for the whole family. The excitement in the casino was contagious, encouraging people to keep sinking money. At the slot machines, players would scream loudly when they hit the jackpot and a pile of tokens. I set a small budget, and kept winning, then losing, then winning, until finally losing a small amount.

His nephew had received $500 for his graduation present, and he lost all except $5 at the Blackjack table. On the way back to his room at night, he decided to try his luck one more time with the $5. He won $800 and wisely stopped there. One never knows if a win will happen again.

Sue, my sorority sister living in Switzerland, asked friends to attend a class reunion at Syracuse University. Most were married, so thinking everyone would bring their husbands, I brought Lee and both of my children. As it turned out, it didn't make a difference as most left their husbands at home, but it became a meaningful experience for my family.

Standing in my old sorority house and wandering the campus brought memories back to me and gave Liz and Ken an early taste of university life. College years were so long ago, in a different life, but I could envision the ghosts of happy times. I hadn't seen my college friends since graduation, and was fascinated to hear about their lives. Another reunion was planned for New York City in 2000.

While there were many laughs with Lee, vast chasms existed between us. The romance was not meant to be forever. I loved learning new things and reading, but he said he had learned all he wanted to know. He would get annoyed if I suggested reading a book. Although he came from a family of teachers, he had dropped out of college to get married young. I cringed when he weaved yarns of untruth about a boat he didn't own, because his ego was uncomfortable around some of my affluent friends.

Several years after the Andy romance ended, I received a letter from him on a Thursday. It asked if I would meet him at the Hyatt Hotel bar to talk the following Sunday. He added, "If you can't make it, just don't show up." Andy knew it wasn't my style to stand someone up, so he thought I would probably take the bait and appear. Control takes many forms. My brother was an example of someone whose control style was blunt and amateurish; Andy was a clever professional. By now, I was wise to his game, so didn't show up.

Winning control is an exhilarating power game between controller and follower. Many controlling people aren't maliciously mean. They just get caught up with the high of their own needs and can't comprehend another point of view. It's also always easier to take control of other people's lives than one's own.

"We love because we need to love, not because we find someone worthy." Finding a suitable mate is the ultimate challenge and adventure. It's one of life's cruel tricks on women that as we get older and more discerning, there are fewer choices. Most gatherings have more single women than men, and men will often date much younger women.

I never thought I would get divorced and wind up single again. Singles parties in middle-age beg the question, "Why did I not find the right companion?" Occasionally a girlfriend gets lucky, giving everyone else hope to chase their dream. However, being single is not one of life's tragedies. Life throws everyone curveballs, and a single life is manageable.

Everyone has emotional baggage, which can be a heavy pile-up by mid-life years. Childhood anger, frustrations and bad habits grow with responsibilities and difficult experiences, creating deep scars as we age. Moreover, people in their fifties and sixties have often lost their physical attractiveness and might be falling apart with various ailments. A common joke is, "Men want a nurse with a purse." When married young, there are many years ahead to enjoy. Later, the scale is tipped, and the healthy years may no longer balance the bad.

Upon rare occasions, an attractive guy with minimal baggage appears on the scene. More often, available single men are somebody else's rejects for a good cause. The remaining selection for both men and women include the controlling, depressed, psychotic, bombastic, the recovering alcoholic, the too fussy, the too vain, the smoker, the slob, the maladjusted and the too old or too young. In addition, there are often conflicting lifestyles, unattractive personality traits and sexual incompatibilities.

Not all men are created equal in the bedroom. An early bad experience can cause an aversion to the opposite sex for life. While sex is easier for men than women, some men selfishly think sex is a woman's duty, others have limitations and are unable to please a woman, and some need coaching. Women need to feel loved and want to please their man, but being a sex object can get old quickly. Consideration and communication are wise if men wish to have a happy relationship.

Traditionally, very little is said about male attributes, while men frequently critique women and their bodies. As women get older, taboos no longer exist, and the oddities of men sometimes provide a good laugh. It can be a shock when personal aspects are not harmonious with the man you see and enjoy. After spending a lot of time getting to know someone, intimacy can be a disappointment.

For centuries, women were forced to accept strict behavior norms plus any marital duty thrust upon them from unpleasant sex to housework. While sometimes it all worked, some women were left disenfranchised. The Women's Movement of the '60s was a freedom call. People can be suppressed, but given the opportunity, they will, of course, choose freedom. The days of a captured wife are over in our civilized world.

After fifty, I've known many attractive single women who lower their bar about who they will date. However, fierce romanticism continues and often resists any assault from reality. Upon rare occasion there is a success story, but I've seen both sexes settle for companionship or convenience.

I looked forward to a night of dancing at the singles' parties. They can be engaging if not attended often or with higher expectations than an evening out. Held in various atmospheric restaurants, clubs, and museum venues, business people and retired older singles mix and mingle. The parties usually provide dancing, appetizers, and entertainment. To my surprise, some singles took the train from Manhattan to attend our local parties. Even the Manhattan scene can feel limited.

I didn't need a man for my identity, and my companion had to be close to suitable. The father of my children had gone bankrupt—leaving me all the bills, so I didn't want someone else to support—and there were lots of those around. Perhaps I was too fussy, but I had to be true to myself, and the attraction had to be mutual. Just as problematic was a man who wanted to travel. My baggage was the need to stay at home with my business and family, so I was not available for many trips.

My friends and I go out for dinner to laugh and commiserate. Realizing that the man of our dreams is unlikely to appear, we keep hoping anyway. The dating situation was frustrating, but we learned to laugh and enjoy our time together. At least past relationships provide entertaining stories, if not a caring companion.

I was blessed with a couple of empathetic, stable, single girlfriends to pal around with in my fifties. Sophia came into my life when she became Rob's roommate and is now often my companion for an outing or party. Elizabeth became extended family when Liz was her daughter's camp counselor and babysitter.

Elizabeth is an attractive blond businesswoman in finance who never married. In her early forties, she bravely adopted a child to raise and support by herself. We were both around the same height and hair color, so were often taken for sisters, although there were definite differences. Elizabeth's manner always reminded me of Judy Woodruff on *PBS News Hour*.

New places always hold the promise of meeting new people. Out of sheer quantity, maybe a good companion will arise. However, it was beginning to seem evident to me that Prince Charming was not in my destiny.

Chapter 28

Teenage Journeys

Raising children provides a chance to relive youth and dream new dreams. It is a mission and challenges to launch them as adults. Liz was a cooperative teenager, but helping her with school entailed relearning geometry and chemistry—challenging tasks that I could have lived without. The reward was to see a young woman with a determination to succeed, a kind heart, and a desire to make the world a better place.

Liz grew and grew, reaching 5' 9½" with a voluptuous body frame that dwarfed my 5' 7" slender physique. She scored very high in abstract thinking and derived energy from others, frequently organizing group gatherings for games or parties. Liz gravitated toward supportive high-achieving friends throughout her middle and high school years. Her various activities included gymnastics, public service for abused women and the school band. Unlike my personality, she loved public speaking and began a well-respected and successful public speaking club.

Graduation in June of 1998 was a true cause for celebration. Liz proved the school advisors wrong by achieving a 3.0 average, overcoming her learning disability and passing all the required math and science classes. Moreover, she received the John Douglas Memorial Public Speaking Award. Difficulties had taught her not to give up, get help when needed, and take neat, copious notes. She would begin college the following September.

We both knew within the hour of our school visit that Marist College was the right place. Highly organized and dynamic teachers provided an impressive presentation at the Open House. The school offered a tutor in one subject per semester to a few select students with documented learning disabilities. Despite the earlier pessimistic predictions by school advisors, Liz's excellent essay, grade point average, and great references from high school earned her admission. Marist was a perfect match for her personality and abilities, offering an excellent opportunity for her to succeed.

As my tutoring years seemed to be ending, I was ready for a vacation. Both children would soon be grown and on their own, so time to travel with Mom was now. I hoped a trip to Europe would widen their perspective on the world, and planned a month-long trip in July of 1998. The final schedule combined a ten-day educational tour group with two weeks of independent travel. Extensive preparation for the independent weeks included guidebooks and faxed reservations. Summer was tourist season, and rooms in smaller lodgings were scarce for three people. A temp administrator with an art director background was hired to check business e-mail and take care of the basics while we were away.

To prepare for museum visits, I had a mandatory family hour before dinner watching "The History of Art," a purchased video series narrated by Sister Wendy. She was a peculiar-looking but brilliant and entertaining nun that I had discovered on PBS. Her special gift for enthusiastically bringing art alive was an ideal introduction to art history. While the mandatory video watching met with opposition initially, everyone agreed after the trip that the knowledge gained enriched their experience. Museums that would have seemed dry and obscure were brought alive by her narrative. Ken would sometimes amaze onlookers by repeating her descriptions while viewing the actual painting.

"A mind that is stretched by a new experience can never go back to its old dimension." – Oliver Wendell Holmes, Jr.

While things we have in common may often join us into a group, travel is an exhilarating mind-opener, valuable for creativity and decision making. I was fascinated by different cultures and customs. Travel had changed my life. I hoped it would give Liz and Ken a new understanding of the world.

A sign held by a friendly cab driver at London's Heathrow Airport greeted our overnight Virgin Air flight from New York. He chatted to our sleepy family about the passing sights while driving on the left side of the street.

The tour group, EF Tours, consisted primarily of teachers and their students, but accepted others to fill the buses. Waiting at our hotel was a high school class with students from Atlanta and a small group of teachers traveling separately. The ten-day tour would travel by bus from England to Paris and then board a train to Barcelona, Spain. Our return flight was scheduled from Rome, two weeks after the tour group departed for the U. S. from Barcelona. We planned two weeks more of independent travel to the French Riviera, Switzerland and Italy.

During the first day in each city, the tour bus driver gave the history and highlights. Then, we hiked for hours and climbed thousands of stairs with our tour guide, Nicki. I came to understand why Nicki taught aerobics during the winter. Fortunately, although in my mid-fifties, I was still in great shape.

The first day in London was a sleepy one, but we kept moving. During the bus tour, the group disembarked at Buckingham Palace where the kids tried to make the guards laugh, St Paul's Cathedral where they learned about its dramatic war history and the Tower of London, famous for its prisoner beheadings. Our following days encompassed the British Museum, the Museum of the Moving Image, a humorous Shakespeare play, an Elizabethan banquet with entertainment, plus a trip to the royal residence of Windsor Castle on the outskirts of London with a fish and chips dinner at a local pub.

From London, the bus drove to Canterbury, England, a picturesque historic town, perhaps best known for the Thomas Beckett beheading. After one day of wandering the city, we embarked aboard a sizeable modern ferry from the White Cliffs of Dover across the English Channel, where another bus waited for our drive to Paris.

Paris exuded all the charm, beauty and adventures we expected. On the first evening, we unexpectedly walked into a red-light district on our way to the Sacre-Couer Cathedral and Montmartre area. I hurried the kids through those busy streets. Crowds were at the cathedral, and many talented sidewalk artists fascinated the onlookers a block away in Montmartre.

Over the following few days, the Paris adventure took us delightful places. The video lessons came to life with the "Mona Lisa" and other masterpieces in the Louvre Museum and impressionist artists such as Monet at the L'Orangerie Museum. Tours of the Fragonard Perfume Factory, Notre Dame Cathedral, then shopping at the Gallery Lafayette and Au Printemps filled our days. Wandering the Champs Elyseé, seeing the Arc de Triomphe and eating delicious French cuisine rounded out the visit.

On the last day, we met up our French au pair, Christelle, at the Eiffel Tower. Hugs and smiles were passed around for a joyous reunion. She showed us a charming, non-tourist bistro for lunch, where we caught up on life events. After saying "au revoir," our visit was capped off that evening with an incredibly stunning boat ride on the River Seine. "The City of Lights" glittered on the banks.

During our travels, there were several memorable "couchette" train experiences. Paris to Barcelona was the first. The couchette sleeping car contained two sets half sheets for our small-sized bunk beds, no running water, and no temperature control. Clara, a Spanish teacher who was traveling with us, volunteered to give backrubs to Liz and me for help sleeping. She was very kind, but our slumber was still broken by the noisy train and its stops. I looked forward to a comfortable night's rest at our hotel in Barcelona. However, Liz had a painful earache the first night, so sleep didn't happen until the doctor arrived and the medicine began to work.

Gaudi's twisting architectural style was sprinkled throughout the city of Barcelona. Our tour bus drove around the town and stopped for an hour at the Gaudi-style Sacrada Familia Cathedral, a complex building that continued under construction for many years. After two days in Barcelona, the tour group's ten-day excursion ended. We bid goodbye and moved to a hotel booked in advance. Ken was taking Spanish at school, so Barcelona seemed an appropriate place to spend a week absorbing the culture.

The new hotel had a large, comfortable room and was easy walking distance to La Rambla, the town's enticing open street strolling area near the beach. Exotic places for tapas, drinks, dramatic Flamenco dance shows and tourist shops called to the pedestrians. On other days, we toured a small museum of Picasso's early artwork and the scenic Parc Guell surrounding Gaudi's home and museum.

The first day trip away from the city was a train to the historic Roman village of Tarragona, with an Archeological Museum to view and a castle's tower to climb. On our last day we embarked on a diversion at the *Port Adventura* amusement park. The kid's brains were getting over-saturated with history and culture, so time for a change. The amusement park was cleverly divided into several countries, each with unique food, rides and ambiance.

We were better prepared for the overnight train to Nice, France, after experiencing the train to Barcelona. This time we slept in our clothes with valuables in a money belt and kept sweatshirts handy for the cold air conditioning.

At sunrise, the laughter of backpacking students awakened us. The group was drinking wine and watching the city lights flicker out as the sun appeared on the French Rivera. We joined the merriment, and I felt like twenty-one again.

The vivid blue waters were a stunning backdrop for Nice, the largest city on the French Rivera. Ken visited a friend from home while Liz and I strolled along the waterfront promenade, toured the shops and enjoyed the tourist resort town. Topless bathers on crowded beaches were a surprise that immediately caught our attention. The following day, we all took a side trip to Monte Carlo in Monaco, legendary for its casinos and the American actress Grace Kelly who became Princess Grace of Monaco. Monaco is the second-smallest sovereign state in the world, after Vatican City. It is widely recognized as one of the wealthiest places in the world.

Sue, my sorority sister from Syracuse, awaited us a short train trip away in Switzerland. She lived with her German husband, Werner, in a lovely suburban Geneva home. We were amazed that her three children fluently switched back and forth among four languages. She said it was a plan from birth. They insisted that the children talk English to their mother and German to their father at the dinner table, so both languages became native tongues. School classes were taught in French, and Spanish was their foreign language at school.

Werner, an attorney working in Geneva, treated us to lunch the next day near his office, where we celebrated Ken's sixteenth birthday. He briefly showed us around the old town and modern city before returning to his office and leaving us to wander.

Chatting later that evening in their garden over fondue was the perfect way to catch up on old times.

With Geneva as a home base, we embarked on a side day trip to the perfectly-manicured Swiss town of Berne. On another day, an exciting funicular cable railway carried us on a ride high up into the Alps to a peak at Rocher de Nayer for a fantastic view. The town of Montreux, well known for its famous summer Jazz festival, was below at the base of the Alps on the Lake Geneva shoreline. While it was the wrong weekend for the music festival, we enjoyed lunch in the town and visited the old Castle at Chillon, memorable by my kids for its dungeons and the toilettes that emptied into the sea.

It was difficult saying goodbye to friends, who wouldn't be seen for a long time, but our days in Europe were limited, and it was a wonderful visit.

As our train arrived in the next city of Venice, Italy, many boat horns honked hello from the canals outside the station. "Vaporetto" boat lines took passengers to stops along the canals, but we quickly found they were undependable as well as noisy. Walking was more enjoyable.

Venice immediately captures the senses, with sights, smells and sounds. Canals wind around historic old buildings and the total absence of cars or modern structures is striking. We did find one storefront McDonald's tucked away down a tiny street on the main floor of an old building, a tiny sign of the modern world. Our charming B&B, perfectly situated near a canal, included an outdoor café serving us a continental breakfast before we strolled to the city's attractions. As an impressive ending to our visit, we watched a massive fireworks display while dining in San Marco Plaza.

We headed southwest on a day train to Florence and were captivated by the picturesque countryside. Memories of Florence as my hometown during the Semester-In-Italy program many years before wistfully returned. My first thought, after getting settled at our hotel, was to locate the Piazza Savonarola again, the location of my college classrooms. The piazza's center statue was ringed by old buildings without any exterior signs. I didn't recognize the entrance, so gave the school's name to a young man on a bike, who showed us the unmarked door. Sadly, only English would come out of my mouth, and I could no longer talk Italian.

Returning to the school with children close to my memory's age seemed almost impossible and made me reflect on the experience. The school had expanded behind the façade, adding an architecture school. Art students were now not only accepted and desirable, but studio classes were available.

Afterward, we jumped from shaded area to shaded doorway in one hundred-degree summer heat while heading to our destinations. I nostalgically mused about the many fun times during those Semester-In-Italy days while wandering the cooler museums and shops.

It was still sweltering hot at our final stop in Rome. The Faulty Towers, our pre-booked English hotel, was based on an English TV sitcom and required a small, rickety elevator shaft ride up five floors. After settling in, we set out to see the city in the late afternoon and evening but were caught in the middle of a bank robbery as we crossed the street. Cops jumped out of police cars with guns drawn right in front of us. I hurried Liz and Ken quickly out of range and through the hustle and bustle of Rome—heading toward the Roman Coliseum where we were to meet our late afternoon walking tour.

The guide told fascinating stories and displayed books that brought the fragmented buildings to life. The current ruins of the Roman Coliseum and other places were covered with transparent overlays depicting the original structure in its time of grandeur. On following days, we joined crowds of tourists at the Vatican and into the Sistine Chapel of St. Peter's Cathedral, and then toured around the many sights of Rome. Strolling through timeless twisting streets and pausing to people-watch ended too soon for me, but Liz and Ken were ready to see their home again. Ciao Italy!

I hoped our European trip gave Liz and Ken a new perspective about the wide-ranging world to bolster future decisions. Ken was searching for answers in a confusing human race. As a brilliant writer and deep thinker, he seemed to derive energy from books and weighty insights, examining every detail and disseminating it to others in a carefully drawn verbal picture. His inquisitive mind explored ideas to their roots and then went forward to the logical results.

Having very high SATs and excellent writing skills gained him acceptance to the Northeastern University business school. Their internship program seemed to be just what was needed to set him on a career path, and the paid intern semesters would help finance the cost of a five-year program.

Chapter 29

The Dotcom Era

Before the office move, Tom Gong, the computer wizard who rented one of my offices, began explaining the future of computers and the internet. He sparked my curiosity by demonstrating it on his computer and explaining the potential. Speeds in 1993 required a lot of patience for slow transmission over the phone lines. The internet was unfamiliar to most everyone. The world had no smartphones, no iPads, no flat-screen TVs, no touch screens, and even no Google.

As the internet gradually became more well-known, it continued to remain drastically different from today. The public still used online dial-up services like AOL, paying for every minute used. Backup storage was on Floppy disks.

In the autumn of 1996, news arrived that the first Internet Trade Show would take place at the Javits Convention Center in Manhattan. I was quick to sign up. Walking down the aisles of booths introducing many emerging technology suppliers generated the realization of my vision. The time had come to launch my business on the internet.

Working from my home was cumbersome. Interviews and presentations required commuting to Manhattan or shipping portfolios. The amazing web could transport images and type effortlessly. Moreover, it could manage our out-of-control resume files and was a perfect way for freelancers to self-enter and update their backgrounds directly. There was no question that the internet could make a huge difference in operations. My brain often felt like a computer flashing "disk is full."

Excited with the new venture, I plunged into the startup opportunity. Early in 1997, I secured the domain name "freelancers.com," then hired a designer and programmer for the website. I searched the internet for major advertising agency names and couldn't find any, but knew it would happen. Google was officially launched the next year in 1998 by two students from Stanford University.

You don't know until you try. Like many other ideas, it seemed simple and wasn't. Breaking new ground without existing models is always challenging, and changing technology makes it more difficult. Potential markets could not be reached until internet speeds improved. I was ahead of my time and had to wait for customers come onboard.

My web launch was disappointing, and the first promotional brochure was quickly outdated. Instead of instant recognition as the first in the field, my great idea limped along and wasn't a recognized star the future. Meanwhile, standard business sales suffered from lack of attention and from not having offices located in Manhattan.

"Life is about timing," said Carl Lewis, the Olympic star.

During our family trip to Europe, my business didn't continue without interruptions as planned. The administrative temp hired to check the e-mail while away had a technical problem during the first week and didn't know how to fix it. Correspondence wasn't answered, and everything piled up waiting for my return.

Sometimes it is difficult to roll the dice and begin the game again. Upon my return from Europe, I was discouraged by the waiting mess and tired of all the responsibility. I went to various headhunters and temp agencies looking for a new career without the headaches. My old friend, Tom Gong, asked me to go into business with him, but his office was on Wall Street in Manhattan. I didn't want the long commute.

A prominent Connecticut recruitment company wanted me to set up their creative temp division, but I was no longer trusting and wouldn't agree to totally give up my illustration business. They felt I would be serving two masters, so we couldn't strike a deal. I couldn't just walk away from everything to become dependent upon another company. If I was out of a job in my fifties, I wanted something to fall back on.

The technology boom started slowly to the visible eye but sprinted out of the gate with amazing speed. A combination of fad-based investing and the abundance of venture capital for startups created the stage, despite the failure of dotcoms to turn a profit. Investors hoped that their companies would one day become profitable, often abandoning a cautious approach for fear of not cashing in on the amazing internet potential.

Unexpectedly, my business began to increase again. "Creative Freelancers" was found on the internet. Companies were installing faster networks, and creative departments became equipped. By the end of 1998, the dotcom era had commenced. Assignments rolled in from all over the country. Several firms expressed merger interest in 1999 but were unwilling to offer any substantial money in return.

Suddenly, the purchase of my internet business was desirable by others. However, the business model needed to be updated and positioned correctly for the mass market. The years 1999 to 2000 were spent preparing my computer infrastructure with a programmer, writing a business plan, and looking for financing or merger opportunities. I simultaneously wrote an integrated sales and accounting program to expedite some internal office systems. An interested investor was ready to sign a deal in December of 2000.

No one in the press or elsewhere saw what would happen next. The stampeding herd of bulls ran off the cliff, and the curtain to opportunity closed as the dotcom bubble broke. My investor wisely walked away to wait for better economic times. Instead of a turnaround, the tragic 911 terrorists' attack followed. The oxygen was sucked out of me. Everything was transformed by circumstances in the blink of an eye. Power, politics and policy are the determining backgrounds for destiny.

"In the business world, the rearview mirror is always clearer than the windshield," said Warren Buffett, the famous business tycoon.

The stock market, which was already suffering from the dotcom bust, plummeted more from the 911 attack. My business came to a standstill. All companies were cutting corners. The creative department is always one of the first budget cuts in a downturn, as the old materials can often be reused. Scandals followed, destroying the public confidence.

My investments also took severe hits. Both of my children were in college with tuition bills needing to be paid, so stocks had to be sold at a low price. Although the business had supplied a good living and I was paying the bills, turning "Creative Freelancers" into a bigger money-maker remained elusive. Experience was a stern teacher, and new limitations had been added to the curriculum. It was a difficult lesson and a breathtaking ride.

Reframing life's disappointments as learning experiences help to cope with the future. Sometimes it can be the catalyst for a new idea. Looking back over my journey, what were the lessons learned and what could have been done differently?

The first thing that comes to mind is I should have removed most of the office doors. Privacy can provide a place to hide from work. One conference room near the reception would have handled most sales meeting needs. Salespeople are best positioned in a glass cubicle near watchful eyes until they prove themselves. An open area is a safe starting place.

I've also learned it's essential to make a sizeable splash early when introducing a new concept so the ripples have the greatest effect possible. Any profitable business will eventually have competition. Don't miss the short window of time when launching an emerging business idea. I thought my business was too "niche" and off the beaten path to attract much money or competition, but I was wrong.

The owner should be visible. Press releases should announce the company launch, speaking events, and industry insights. Create a buzz. Speaking platforms at luncheons are an ideal low budget way to spread your message. People want to be entertained. Talking honestly about your business and occasionally injecting some humor will work best. Toastmasters International is helpful, if not a natural for the task.

Don't just hope a big net will catch the preferred fish. Target your audience carefully. Unless the salesperson has an account in their network, advertising is faster. Ads reach more territory than calls. The internet and social media provide infinite opportunities in today's world.

Take time to network. Each person that you reach reaches more people. A beneficial company image must be projected to get the sale, but networking's biggest draw will be from personal connections. Others can identify with vulnerability. No one changes anyone's mind by shouting or holding up a sign, but they do by speaking from the heart.

Accountability is critical. Give incentives for results, and don't forget to applaud a job well done. I should have asked for dated weekly sales reports and all records containing contact interaction, especially for the first six months of employment—as contact records can get lost and are easy to bluff.

Check references. Good people will often get praise. I usually checked but was more flexible about sales skills because some can transition well from other positions to sales. However, friendly account people will sometimes apply for sales because they need a job, expressing hope more than ability. At the interview, agree to sales goals. If not achieved, make clear their job position would be in jeopardy.

Protect your important records. They could be sold to the competition. Utilize non-compete contracts with specific time limits or appropriate territories. Always watch out for rats in disguise. Early ancestors of the human mammal line were small rat-like creatures. Predator instincts remain strong in some people.

Know your employees. Win, a friend and professor of psychology from Columbia, described humans as divided into three major groups: those that need power, those that need to achieve, and those that need affiliation. Most personalities are dominated by one of those needs. I looked for achievers.

Develop a personal sales style. Be memorable and sincere. Bernie was compassionate and knew how to ask questions carefully, then not hang up until he made his point and set a time to follow-up. Rob's style was being a showman and making people laugh, talking about some mutual interest, or laughing about events.

Continue to interact. The owners' voice will hold the most weight. Maintain a communication that explores your top client needs. Stop all the noise and concentrate on what is important. Utilize weekly reports from employees for their comments and updates. Don't just give the pitch and then leave the leads to others.

Work wisely. The Golden Rule, "Do to others as you want them to do to you," is often not the right approach in a business. If everyone acted by that ideal principle, it would be a better world. However, some people will lie, cheat and kill to get what they want. High ideals and goals have to be tempered with realistic expectations, just as our dreams have to grow with opportunities available.

Partner if possible. A financial partner who understands general business is wise, unless you have a very advantageous alternative. Giving part of the business away can be well worth it for a jump start. Of course, be on guard with a written contract. Never invest everything. Have a good back-up plan.

When you have your own business without a partner, no one is there to help problem solve and reinforce potential business plans. Strength and enjoyment have to come from working at something you genuinely believe in. The financial success and entrepreneur adventure would have been much more satisfying for me with a supportive person.

The first person to have the emerging idea should reap the rewards. That person has to work fast with a good plan. Only one in three startups last beyond the first three years—a discouraging statistic.

Learning opportunities to improve chances of success are available in schools and online. In a world run by technology you have to compete. First, explore and learn, then go in with your dreaming eyes wide open. A majority of entrepreneurs never received a bachelor's degree. Many owners are not startup pioneers of unique ideas but pioneer a new marketplace. Some just add their personality to an existing product or shop, fashioning new markets. My friend Pam, with her wicker shop, is an example.

Deciding when to sell the business can also be tricky. Like the stock market, sell when high. Two friends from my symphony group, Regina and Joern, came to the United States from Germany without assets. They worked very hard as shipping brokers while raising a family. When the economy turned in their favor, they wisely decided to take the earnings to retire early—investing in passive real estate and a comfortable life.

My dream of adventure and romance grew beyond my wildest expectations. Life has propelled me into the unimaginable. I still remember my existential inner self watching my human body in the heyday of my Manhattan office. As men came with requests and questions, I wondered, "How did I get here?"

Chapter 30

2000 Surprises

Cameras flashed as the year changed from 1999 to 2000. Instead of the many newspaper photographers that were at my grandparent's turn-of-the-century wedding in 1900, midnight in the year 2000 produced flashes from cell phone cameras in my living room. The celebration and excitement about the new century came to pass with close friends at a small black-tie New Year's Eve dinner party in my condo. Jane and John, Pat and Ray, Stephanie and Bob, Elizabeth and a few others attended. As the Times Square ball dropped on TV, we blew horns and kissed each other with warm wishes for happiness. The "Y2K" year had begun. A new century of surprises awaited our hopeful group of people.

Jane and John, a couple from our symphony group dinners, seemed to have the perfect life. They often hosted our parties in their lovely home, which looked out on a colorful garden in the summer. Both were gracious, kind people. Jane's appearance always reminded me of the movie actress Sally Fields. John was a handsome, successful attorney who insisted on doing the dishes and being helpful. Although Jane had both a law and a psychology degree, she had given up a career to raise their family. Their children were close in age to Liz and Ken, so we attended senior shows and school functions together.

Bad things shouldn't happen to good people. In July 2000, John tragically died of pancreatic cancer. I struggled with accepting the surprise diagnosis when I learned of it a couple of months before his death. The world needed more people like him. Perhaps the only benefit of knowing someone is dying is the chance to say what they meant to you. It was a difficult call to make, but I expressed gratitude to him for his kindness, said he was in my prayers, and told him about my early memories. Always a gentleman, John expressed appreciation for reaching out to him and never complained.

Our symphony group thought they knew him well but were surprised to learn about his amazing professional life at the funeral service. Some of his friends from the legal department of a major accounting firm hailed him as the "moral compass" of the company. He was frequently consulted about questionable issues and ethics. Two Jewish business associates spoke eloquently about him at a Catholic Mass for this Scottish Protestant man. They said his integrity, judgment and manners were a lesson to them all.

They established a memorial Trust in his memory, which provided scholarship money to attend Harvard Law School for a promising student who embodied the same ethical qualities. While the age of 61 is too young to die, he left a meaningful legacy and will be missed by many. As friends pass from life, it reinforces the need to appreciate existing connections.

Nostalgia for the past met with hope for the future as the century changed. More reunions seemed to happen. Memories come flooding back as we learn about how our friends' lives unfold. Relationships glue the episodes of our life together.

Our second sorority reunion took place in August of 2000. Unsure of recognizing people and hesitant to walk up to strangers, sorority sisters gathered on either side of the big clock at the Roosevelt Hotel in Manhattan until it struck noon. Familiar faces came alive as the clock struck the hour—followed by a lot of hugs, before heading to a classmate's penthouse apartment near the United Nations for our pizza party event.

Although I had lived in Manhattan for many years, I had never taken an official tour or viewed it as a tourist. Most in our group were first-time tourists so we all took the Circle Line boat tour around Manhattan the next day, with a guide giving the history about places of interest. The Statue of Liberty, holding a giant torch, was an inspiring spectacle from the boat view below. It was easy to see how the towering image of "Lady Liberty" ignited the imagination of early immigrants arriving by ship.

During the five years between our reunions, two sorority sisters had died, one of a brain tumor and the other of cancer. Before the advent of e-mails or cell phones, it was complicated to stay in touch by writing letters or making costly long-distance phone calls. Preoccupied with daily circumstances, the loudest voice is heard, and friends are taken for granted. Good friends faded from my mind without realizing their role in my life. Without long-term companions, life becomes sound and video bites, lacking an anchor or script. Years later, the whole picture emerges.

A second tourist opportunity happened on Labor Day Weekend of 2001 when my niece and her husband visited from Ohio. It was a perfect autumn weekend in Manhattan, and I felt like "Auntie Mame"—showing my out-of-town family a world they didn't know existed. Manhattan amazes everyone with its sights and sounds. First-timers stare in astonishment at the endless tall buildings reaching into the sky and the busy streets filled with thousands of people.

Niece Deborah, a business executive and a teacher, had married a country boy. Sid, Deborah's husband, was from the rural Midwest and expected the worst of New York from movie depictions. Sid could find his way out of the wilderness with the skill of an indigenous Indian, but he had a massive fear of large cities like New York. He was a charming guy with great story-telling ability, a large build and a friendly smile.

Working and living in Manhattan for so many years had left me blind to the small enjoyments of a tourist. We first walked from our meeting place in Bryant Park into Grand Central Station. Busy commuters hurrying in different directions with their briefcases had to be navigated until we exited through a large, impressive gourmet market with the biggest shrimp anyone had ever seen.

All eyes lit up as we wandered past the Helmsley Palace Hotel, onto posh Park Avenue, and through the magnificent St. Patrick's Cathedral. After a light lunch at Au Bon Pain, we wandered to Rockefeller Center, NBC Studios, Radio City Music Hall and Broadway—

with an incredible sea of multi-cultural people and entertaining street actors. A quick subway ride took us from 42nd Street to Fulton near the South Street Seaport, where a unique indoor-shopping building was full of aquatic items and souvenirs. Boats were in the harbor, and the sidewalk was filled with magicians and painters.

On the trip back, our train stalled, so we took a longer route that involved train changes with a lot of walking underground. Sid had never been on a subway before, but he became a well-seasoned commuter in the tunnel passageways, by the end of the day,

Gondolas on a lake in Central Park floated past our outdoor table while we indulged ourselves in gourmet dining that evening at the Boat House Restaurant. Central Park, often pictured in movies as a nighttime death trap, was pleasantly safe. After dinner, we joined the strolling pedestrians on a dark path lit by streetlamps. A cop car was noticeably parked on the road but not needed. Sid came away loving New York. I'm sure his friends thought differently about the city after he brought his adventures to life with animated humor.

Two weeks later, the 911 terrorist attack struck terror in the nation. Not since the Cuban missile crisis had everyone been so frightened. Personal tragedies from the building collapse hit many people in New York and surrounding areas. Sadly, my roommate Sandra's first husband and some local Greenwich families were disaster victims. The millions who read the *New York Times* op-eds about the victims were captivated by fascinating episodes from these ordinary lives. Actual life chapters can be more intriguing and imaginative than any fiction writer could conceive.

Every lifetime is affected by world events. As a child in the 1950's, I hid under school desks at atomic bomb drills and watched the McCarthy era witch-hunt against Communists. The 1960s brought the Cuban Missile Crisis, Kennedy's assassination, and an American landing on the moon. Numerous protests filled the streets over the Viet Nam war, women's liberation, and racial discrimination. When my business was launched in the early 1970s, interest rates were a high 13%, Jimmy Carter was President, and our country's unemployment was high.

The decade continued with Ayatollah Khomeini rising to power in 1979, deposing the Shah of Iran and holding fifty U.S. embassy officials as hostages for a tense year. As an adult, I cheered the fall of the Berlin Wall in 1989. Then the "Camp David Accord" was signed between Israel and the Arabs, giving a short false sense of peace and prosperity in the nineties.

The Mideast has been a continuous hotspot during my lifetime, and no end seems in sight. Now we live in an age of terrorism and hear marchers chant, "Death to America." Ordinary people just want to live their lives in peace and harmony but wonder, "What will happen next?"

Chapter 31

Today's View

We are spectators, participants or thrill takers in the game of life. Entrepreneurs have to be willing participants or thrill takers. A high threshold for rollercoaster rides is needed. Surprises wait at every corner, and letdowns have to be accepted as an opportunity to reinvent plans for the better. Previous failures increase an entrepreneur's chance of success the next time.

Not everyone is cut out for it. Moreover, skills and opportunities have to first converge in a unique way to provide the occasion. Taking the plunge into your own business can be daunting, but you don't know until you try. No job is secure.

Statistics about entrepreneurs are blurry. However, about 20% of new companies fail in their first year. Some may never get off the ground or may make avoidable mistakes. By the fifth year, there is a 50% failure rate; 19% fail because of too much competition, and another 18% because of pricing or cost issues. Always have a plan A and B.

Those that are driven by passion and commitment are most likely to succeed. It takes a willingness to observe, listen and learn—plus strong leadership and discipline. Other frequent reasons for failure are listed as taking advice from the wrong people, lacking good mentorship and lack of capital. Company founders were 125% more successful if they had worked previously in a similar industry.

Don't be scared out of your dream. There are many winners, and I consider myself among them. In the United States, small businesses comprise 99.9% of all the country's firms and employ close to 50% of the workforce. Moreover, small business creates over 60% of the new jobs.

The superstars are the most visible, but all small business people can make an immense difference in their own communities. The over 400 million entrepreneurs worldwide create most of the world's new jobs. They provide income, purpose and self-worth to billions of people.

It is notable that over 50% of small businesses start out running from someone's home. Every salesperson and freelancer is a startup, bravely facing daily survive-or-die challenges. Sometimes they grow into a larger thriving business with employees. Design studios, store owners and real estate salespeople all have to explore for prospects and entice customers.

The U.S. leads the world with venture capital startups. The success of those companies is mainly attributed to leadership. The leader must build a strong team and drive a business model with focused discipline. They are skills needed by all small business owners as well.

Today's women take for granted what was off-limits for my generation. Opportunities are now there, but it still takes careful planning, focus and work. Networking forums, skill classes and finance sources can be found online, at schools and at the library. Industry think tanks, venture capital companies dedicated to women, and women mentors can open doors.

Liz helped to manufacture her luck by having an upbeat, positive attitude and making good decisions along the way. Her hard work and survival skills won out over a learning disability. We thought teaching elementary school would be the perfect major because she has a knack for handling kids. Once in college, however, she chose a political science major and public relations minor. She loved public speaking, taking charge, working in school government, and participating in the Marist Polls. For a junior year internship, she was offered a position with the famous TV newsman, Gabe Pressman, at *NBC* in New York City, a job she couldn't and didn't refuse. When an opportunity shows up, grab the ball and go for the goal.

Senior year, she was elected Senior Class President and Senate Speaker. It brought tears to my eyes seeing her at center stage at graduation, wearing the special President's drape. The high school teacher's predictions were very wrong, and Liz's impossible dream had come true.

Events in life often shift like the weather. One day can be sun and the next a storm. On graduation day, May 18, 2002, it poured rain and then snowed in the early morning, setting new weather records. Practice the day before had been clear skies and warm. The outdoor procession for handing out diplomas had to be canceled, and everything moved at the last minute into the gym. Due to lack of space, only two parents were allowed into the graduation observance. Becky, Dougal, Laura and Ken drove to Poughkeepsie for the occasion, and Rob came in my car. I stood with Rob for a shortened, noisy ceremony, and other guests had to watch on close circuit TV or miss it entirely. The only saving grace was watching the excitement and enthusiasm of the graduates who had worked so hard to earn their special day, and of course, seeing my daughter Liz finally achieving her dream.

Although anticlimactic for the parents, the graduates were happy. They celebrated with parties in warm, sunny weather all senior week and just wanted their diplomas. Parents chipped in for a luncheon back at Liz's townhouse, and all rejoiced together. Sunshine arrived in time for party photos, and a videotape of the entire ceremony was mailed to the parents by the school.

Despite a poor job market in 2002, a *Washington Post* ad led Liz to a supervisor position for the Congressional Page Program at the House of Representatives. Unfortunately, since 911, there's always been the fear of terrorist attacks, so she learned how to use a gas mask and went into lockdown when a sniper hit the DC area. Anywhere can be a terrorist target, and the government has more security than most places. The job is mostly on evenings and weekends, so those hours afford experimentation with volunteer activities and charities during the day. She is now considering enrolling for an MBA degree.

On Ken's first night at Northeastern University, he was mugged coming home from a party at 3 a.m. He fortunately only received a bloody nose and wasn't seriously injured. It made him more careful in the future. Ken's first year went smoothly with good grades. He joined a fraternity with strong scholastic and community values along with his freshman roommate.

Northeastern University was unique at that time because it offered business students four semesters of internships. After a full first year of classes, the semesters would alternate between internship and classes to complete a five-year degree. After three days working on his internship at an investment banking firm, I received a call saying, "The job is great!" With a goal in sight, Ken was transformed into an adult. He arrived at the office for 8:30 a.m. analyst meetings, and thoroughly enjoyed the interactions on assignments. His VP boss was a wonderful mentor, who provided opportunities to grow, introduced him at business luncheons, and took him to big league ball games.

Then the 911 terrorist attacks dramatically changed corporate budgets the following year. The company would no longer pay interns, so they offered a Series 7 exam sponsorship instead of money. He jumped at the opportunity, scoring higher than most seasoned professionals on the six-hour exam. An enjoyable, high-paying career seemed within grasp. Ken is even talking about attending graduate school.

Despite a few setbacks, both of my children seem to be thriving and growing into competent adults with strong personalities and distinctive talents. Neither is confrontational nor argumentative unless in self-defense.

Some things don't materialize as expected. I've tried to stay in touch with my stepdaughters, but they have their own busy lives. After our separation, Rob was jealous that I had a good relationship with them. He made it clear that I had my family, and he had his. Rather than create more trouble and work for myself, I didn't push the relationships. They were always welcome but usually just visited their father in Manhattan. In the earlier years, I acted as a buffer to their father's insensitivity and tried to instill more normal family values into their lives. I had hoped it would lead toward a long-term, friendly family. Now I step back and let the arguments happen.

Laura and Jennifer are in Boston, and Allie is on Martha's Vineyard. They see their father from an adult woman's point of view and they wonder how I could have married him. I usually stay with Laura when I visit Boston, and we communicate the most. We chat and laugh for hours—as she has a great sense of humor. Laura always has a boyfriend, but no Mr. Right. She is currently working as a computer graphic artist at an architectural firm and keeps very busy with activities and friends. On Thanksgiving, Laura compassionately serves dinner to the homeless. When Liz graduated from college, she was the only one of the sisters who made the trip over to the Marist graduation ceremony.

Jennifer has been civil and distant, still resentful that I did not agree with her views. She worked for many years handling workers' compensation claims in a corrupt and sexist office. *Hustler* magazines were all over, and the men went to lap dancing bars instead of audits. After accumulating evidence on scandalous and illegal behavior, she threatened to report them. They offered her a large settlement not to talk. Figuring it would be a lengthy court battle against an old boy's network, she took the settlement and is now trying to find a new career in her mid-forties.

Allie finally threw Gary out of the Martha's Vineyard house with his father's consent. The drinking binges had never stopped. When the grandfather became terminally ill, Allie didn't know how any of his immediate family would treat her living situation in the house when he died. A fortuitous interview at a new radio station changed her life with a job and romance. It was love at first sight when she met Roy. Within three months, they announced their engagement and were married the following October. Roy's mother owned an attractive estate on the Vineyard and a vacation home in Europe. His father was an Episcopalian minister. His parents were divorced.

It was a charming wedding on a picture-perfect day. The sister of Allie's mother had the title "mother of the bride." It was a natural choice. However, her aunt insulted me in a random comment, for no apparent reason, insinuating I'd done nothing to be considered the mother. I didn't answer but knew all the emotion and effort I had put into a stable home life. I don't recall her aunt ever paying a visit, and she rarely seemed in touch. The aunt should have been appreciative and gracious—not condescending. I just steamed inside quietly.

As a man, Rob often got the credit for my family's stable home life. Most assumed he put up some child support and partially paid their college costs. While I've kept my emotions in check, anger and frustration were often in my heart on his Sunday visits. The fires that festered inside me were never allowed to emerge. While I've tried to forgive and forget, I am still dealing with his problems. The embers remain lit. Much more compassionate men have been alienated from their children.

Today, Rob is a lonely, broke old man, a shadow of the successful entertaining guy who always got his way. Despite all the smoking and drinking, his body is surprisingly strong. However, his memory is deteriorating, and one eye has macular degeneration. He complains a lot and wants people to pay attention to his ailments but doesn't get much sympathy. Earlier, there was no compassion for me when I needed it, so I am numb to his whines. People get what they give out in life.

Dougal and Becky always visit my condo on Thanksgiving, and Rob is invited. They are an excellent example of a successful marriage. Becky has had a prosperous career as an oil trader, but significant economic changes have her looking for a new career. She is a talented saleswoman, so she is thinking about reinventing herself for real estate.

My Aspen ski buddies had a spontaneous reunion at Joan's home in Manhattan when Mary Lou and her husband John decided to visit New York from Texas for the NYC Bike Marathon. I didn't participate in the marathon but joined their "pasta energy party" the night before. Mary Lou still has her entertaining wit. She had married John while in New York and moved to Texas for his job. Always an adventurer, she has traveled all over the world and encouraged her two children to do the same. Her family has taken several foreign exchange students into their Austin, Texas home, developing an extended family from different countries. Back in Texas, she runs a small marketing firm. Joan married a criminal attorney who became police commissioner. Their children are doing well.

Most every weekend, Joan and her family go to their chalet near a small ski resort.

I was inspired to go skiing again, so Ken and I took a trip to southern Vermont. It was a cold weekend on the mountain, around twenty degrees with sheets of pearl-gray "boilerplate ice" on the trail. I made it clear that I only wanted to ski intermediate trails since I hadn't skied in a long time. After a while, Ken got bored and asked if I would do an advanced slope, so I agreed, and it went well. The next slope he headed down was an expert double black diamond trail. I didn't read the sign. At the top, I fell into a long slide over moguls down a steep trail. My skis remained on for the entire distance rendering my knee twisted but not broken. The injury required a ski patrol sleigh ride down the mountain and about six months of healing to feel better. That was my last skiing trip.

I haven't seen my brother since my father's death in 1986, but I am close to his daughters. Both Joanne and Deborah visit when they can, and we chat on the phone. They are intelligent, kind, young women who remind me of my mother.

Plans can be derailed by romance. If women get attached to a man without long-range planning, the relationship can become a dead end. Prince Charming is elusive for some and drains resources for others. My niece Joanne has been living with the wrong man for nine years. After interning in my Manhattan office and finishing her art degree, she met an attractive jewelry designer at an art festival. Jason is a nice-looking, easy-going guy, so I can see how it started. She didn't expect it to last but grew to love him. He proceeded to derail any stable career plans for several years and spent her credit card into heavy debt. Joanne now works at a healthcare agency, paying most of the bills and loan expenses.

For Christmas every year, my brother sends a box of chocolates. Candy hurts my teeth, so I've never been a candy person, but my guests enjoy it, and it is a thoughtful gesture. Then he calls to chat, so I thank him for the candy, and we have a civil discussion. He is not an evil person. We just don't click, and I left him out of my emotions years ago. I don't want him to try to control me again or experience any conflicts from a new relationship.

I was surprised to learn that he still had control over me when Sharon, my Manhattan roommate from the early 1970s, visited New York City last spring. She is now Dr. Sharon G, a family psychologist practicing in California. Although we stayed in touch with Christmas cards and phone calls, I hadn't seen her since she left for graduate school after the wedding with Alex. During the day, we visited Ground Zero, where the World Trade Center was destroyed, then walked north through SoHo and Greenwich Village.

Sharon's passion is horseback riding, and she owns a horse. "My family therapy business helps to support my expensive equestrian hobby." Alex was ranked as the top person in regional sales management for his company and talks about taking an early retirement package in a few years. It will leave him financially comfortable, so he plans to buy a business.

After a delightful dinner, I jokingly asked Sharon for a professional opinion, "Why wasn't I able to find the right relationship?"

She quickly inquired, "What do you remember about men during the first two years of life?" Although it seemed incredibly early to have much effect on my life, my taunting brother was the only male that came to mind. I didn't think my brother had affected my self-confidence until that moment. That bit of knowledge changed the future. I refused to be intimidated by public speaking in front of groups. I just got angry at his controlling nature when I felt nervous, and it worked.

An awareness of the driving forces can lead to mastering weaknesses—far better to face those dark ghosts of our past. Grudges and anger destroy us. Identifying, forgiving and forgetting toxic people should be a goal.

The sea has been relatively calm for a while now. Society desperately wants to become whole again, but many looming uncertainties exist. Thankfully, I am still financially stable, and my childrearing job is almost over. Others have told me that children come back with adult problems later, but I am enjoying the empty nest for now.

The Women's Gathering at church is a special place. Someone tells the story of her life while we enjoy a potluck dinner in a member's home. Stories range from abuse and sickness to riches and fame. There have been tears of laughter and watery eyes for sadness. Although very diverse in personalities and affluence, the women create a common bond by understanding that we face common hurdles as women.

As I began writing for the group talk, there was too much to say in just a half-hour. I gave a short talk, but it became much more. Quiet nights provided an after-dinner conversation with the pages of a journal. The process identified a deep need to share my life with someone. My companion has been a collective voice from ghosts of the past. Words come from those who taught me lessons or passed on their ideas. Assembling the stories in a tangible manner was a form of self-analysis. I wrote thinking it would be reading entertainment for my senior years.

A coherent image was produced from the puzzle pieces, and a fateful vein appeared in the narrative. Predictions have come true. I knew there would be a reason for the guiding light of my memory bank. Now I have the experiences in my writings. A curious spirit is still inquiring.

Chapter 32

Sparks, Choices and Coincidences

I was sitting outside in my backyard last night, looking at the stars, listening to the crickets and seeing where my inquiring mind would go. I've found thoughts will ruminate mentally without direction until ready and then blossom into a matured concept or action. Inspiration is born of stillness. Plateaus percolate ideas. Sometimes, if we listen carefully, sparks of energy will lead, or calls will come from beyond, inviting us to a special destiny. The universe can often provide definite messages.

Chemistry is not just a buzzword. It's been proven that the average human at rest produces around 100 watts of power. It is the glue that brings us together as we interact. An inner energy drives our ability to network for social and business connections—ultimately affecting our path.

Simple sparks from a facial expression will transfer an idea, create a magnetic attraction and empower personalities. An angry tone of voice, a warm laugh or a handshake can convey a message.

Events converge, becoming a signpost to follow. Perhaps a decision by others will change our life.

My mind keeps returning to early memories, trying to make sense out of it all. Some probabilities about our future exist in our genes. Then random world events and choices happen on our path. Could the random interactions be part of a more significant intention? Are the coincidences that occur in our lives part of a path set in motion before we act? When odds are against it, the line blurs between coincidence and destiny.

Hit and miss events also exist in the subatomic realm. That science is very different from our touchable world. The physical dimension of matter comes in and out of existence. Nanotechnology is the computation system of probabilities from a non-material realm. The starting point, somewhere beyond matter, leaves room for many explanations. It could be a way for the spiritual to enter the physical. Is the brain just a lens for another dimension?

A concept named "The String Theory" attempts to bring the larger physical world together with the subatomic for a unified theory of the universe. Still unresolved, the working formulas indicate multiple parallel universes. I do not see multiple universes as a conflict with religion. The Bible says, "In my Father's house there are many rooms." Where we draw the line for our beliefs is a personal decision.

There is an undeniable complexity of the human spirit. I frequently feel like a pawn in a larger plan. While not suggesting that there is a grand puppeteer micromanaging our lives, I suggest there is a powerful spiritual dimension that cannot be measured or predicted. Where science stops, the eternal power of God takes over.

Early life memories, dreams, senses, Wade's voice after death, converging events and predicted fortunes all lead to my belief in a spiritual component behind the physical world. I've experienced enough glimpses to believe in an eternal soul.

Thoreau wrote, "When you are born, your work is placed in your heart." Non-verbal thoughts can ignite the future, as thoughts can be expressed by many languages. Lifestyles can determine if disease genes will get turned on. Each person can avoid or fulfill many genetic predispositions by their choices. We are not defined by fate, but it intervenes, limiting pathways and opening doors. We are made from the material of the universe, but no other creature on earth has the capacity to make symphonies out of random notes.

A teacher friend of mine commented after her daughter was grown, "I could have saved myself twenty years of frustration because my difficult daughter wouldn't have turned out any different." I have also seen parents' efforts make an immense difference, but the child has to be willing. Ultimately each individual shapes their own fate.

"Choices are the hinges of destiny." —Edwin Markham, American poet.

We wonder, "How can I make a wise choice?"
Should we react to a spark, or might it be toxic?
Turning points often have difficult decisions. Visions unfurl slowly over time. I've found refusing to be the victim, taking control of the cards and playing the perceived best choice is the decision with least regret. Mistakes may be made derailing the journey of our dreams, so be ready to reinvent. Focus on the goal and

leave harmful choices quickly. We often have to see what we don't want, before clear goals materialize. Limitations and depression are the walls we must all pass through.

Owning a business is like having a child. It's very difficult to give up after all the nurturing infused. A similar progression to raising children is happening with my business. When children are born, they seem destined to realize all your unfulfilled dreams. As their personalities develop, strengths and weaknesses appear. I feared an empty nest, but after high school, an empty nest was needed relaxation. I am now ready to cruise a little with my business and want less tension in my life.

After having a successful business in Manhattan for twenty-five years, I currently enjoy working out of my home. At least two hours a day are gained by not commuting to New York, and stormy weather is never a problem. I get a good night's sleep and wash my hair or exercise before beginning work. Communication by telephone or e-mail is comfortable, and there are always clients to call. Most every day at 9 a.m., I head to my home office, a habit strengthened by many years of practice. However, there is now the freedom to enjoy entertaining activities and look forward to retirement.

I've re-programmed my dreams again and gave "Creative Freelancers" a new internet rebirth at "IllustratorsOnline.com." It is less complex and more manageable for my retirement years.

"Freelancers.com" still exists, but it is difficult to compete with the new low-price bidding sites. Customer service is pushed to the side in favor of bargains with automation. I am still hoping to sell part of the business, perhaps the name or database of thousands.

As I look back, the Fulbright scholar from India saw many complex lines in my palm and correctly predicted a strong career that separated later into two parts, a late marriage, multiple children, child with a difficult problem, numerous flirtations, a late life romance and a very "interesting" life. They have all come to pass.

When I had inquired about money, I was told that I would be reasonably comfortable but not achieve great wealth. He also said to be careful in my early 60s, as there was a sign that something grave would happen, in ancient times meaning "death at sea."

The second psychic's predictions came when I was newly pregnant with Ken. The predictions matched earlier readings about my career and a few new ones were added: I would have a son, there would be many lawyers in my life, and I would enjoy living out of the city in perhaps two different places. She repeated the ominous warning to be careful of danger after sixty.

A son was born, there were many lawyers in my life, and I moved out of Manhattan to Connecticut. As predicted, I've had a financially comfortable life, but I could never achieve great wealth.

Both fortune-tellers warned me about my sixties. I would like to think that exact foretelling of the future is improbable, and if not, that those dangers are already past. However, I confess the fear has made me somewhat hesitant to travel over water. I'm getting all the standard tests and check-ups to play it safe. Time will tell. We live full of questions, and the role of fate is one of them. Standing in the anteroom to old age with dire predictions about the age sixty creates a quiet apprehension. I am in good health and will deal with whatever comes my way as usual.

I peruse photos and think about the few cherished possessions from my childhood that remain. The under-dress to Mom's wedding gown and some black lingerie from her trousseau are still with me. Although I remember her with some added pounds, the dress fits my slender figure like a glove. A thin gossamer fabric covered her fitted, elegant silk slip that I could still wear as a gown.

Her bedroom furniture was always captivating. As a child, I would brush my fingertips over the patterns of the inlaid wood of her intriguing, elegant dresser from the 1930s. The pattern was beautiful, while the drawers held special treasures. It was all part of a grown-up mystique. I liked to watch her sitting at the mirror combing her brunette hair or using a little powder and rouge. Occasionally, I would get to sit in front of the mirror as she used a curling iron on my straight hair to create a popular style for young girls. The bedroom set was what I longed to inherit more than anything else in the house. Now it is in my room, filling my life with memories. Mom is still with me.

Shakespeare wrote, "We know what we are, but know not what we may be." My adventures have taken me on quite a ride to a place I never imagined. An occasional ghost comes floating back to me, ignited by the flicker of a candle, a passage in a book, or a favorite photo. A flame might evoke the memory of laughing friends around a dinner table or a fun moment with a romantic illusion. A book passage about two young girls traveling around Manhattan recalled my early explorations of a sparkling Manhattan that pulsed with possibilities. There are many fond memories of joyful experiences filled with excitement and warmth, and some shocking, fateful events. The "writing on the wall" has often clearly called me to the next plateau.

All lives are personal mystery stories. Watching the clues unfold creates surges of excitement and passion. Reaching for the stars can bring wonderful surprises.

In school, I followed attainable short-term goals, hoping they would lead somewhere exciting. It led to blundering down some wrong paths teaching what to avoid along the way. Agonizing over past mistakes is futile, so I learned it was better to live in the moment and keep trying. It has been wisely said, "Our greatest glory is not in never falling, but in rising every time we fall." I'm the same child, but with a better ability to weigh events and come to conclusions. The years provide a wider angle for examining how the cards were played.

Being forty was hard to imagine, and now sixty has arrived. My latest companion, a nice guy escaping from some of his own problems, sent roses for my sixtieth birthday. I am the first person he is dating after a failed marriage. That situation rarely works out, and we have several conspicuous differences. Whatever may happen, some good conversations providing mutual needed support are shared.

Floating balloons above a dozen roses enliven my day as flashbacks race through my mind. The bonus years have arrived. I think of after sixty as the bonus years because more doors will close, life's driving forces diminish, and declining health is known to take a toll. I continue to admire people who handle life's challenges well. While I still dream of "setting the world on fire" and have the ambitions of twenty-something, the clock is ticking.

It has been an extraordinary journey. I miss some elements from the past very much but some wisdom has been gained. Words left by kind people still endure.

We live in a world of disorder and conquest, yet beauty and grace. We awake to see gorgeous flowers, live with those we love, watch stunning sunsets, and marvel with amazement. Opportunities await.

If destined to be an entrepreneur, develop the skills, explore your interests, and listen carefully to the universe. Your path will arise.

No matter what the future holds for me, it has been a journey of discovery with no misgivings.

I have loved and lost,
Laughed and cried, then laughed again,
Followed my dreams to unimaginable adventures,
Had the courage to accept life's curveballs,
Faltered but fulfilled the tasks put before me.
Turned the spark of opportunity into a
thriving business,
Filled my niche as a businesswoman,
Listened carefully to the universe,
Tried my utmost, and played life's cards
the best I could.

EPILOGUE

The next decade was full of surprising events. It began with an exciting new romance, but then the surging waves rolled in. While I didn't experience the "death at sea" as seen in the ancient sign, the storm was intense for two years and was very wet. A huge flood in my home necessitated walls being ripped out, and one floor completely redone. Concurrently, serious family illnesses beset my ship. My dear niece Deborah became permanently crippled from the horrible disease of CIDP. Ex-husband Rob died surrounded by dementia predicaments. I semi-retired and was drowning in the stress of multiple problems.

Then the sun came out, and good times were happening again. A relaxing trip to New Hampshire, researching my father's roots and a trip to Ohio, meeting some of my brother's family for the first time brought joy. Old age changes people, and my brother unexpectedly apologized for not treating me well when we were young. He went out of his way to do whatever I asked during the visit.

The psychic had said there was a chance of two home moves, but I didn't plan on leaving Manhattan, much less departing Greenwich CT. Regina's invitation to her Florida condo, plus a long, hoped-for but surprise sale of my freelancers.com name again supplied the "writing on the wall." The end of the decade brought a move to Florida with fun-filled women's clubs, worthwhile charity work, and the delightful opportunity to become an avid ballroom dancer.

AUTHOR'S NOTE

The story and all the characters in this book are real, but it bears mentioning that I have used some pseudonyms in order to protect privacy.

Please write a customer review.

www.TheWriteWall.com

Made in United States
Orlando, FL
20 August 2023

36270153R00163